Overcoming Math Anxiety

Randy Davidson

———

Ellen Levitov

University of New Orleans

HarperCollins*CollegePublishers*

Sponsoring Editor: Anne Kelly
Assistant Sponsoring Editor: Lisa Kamins
Project Editor: Cathy Wacaser
Design Administrator: Jess Schaal
Cover Design: Kay Fulton
Cover Illustration: Patti Green
Printer and Binder; Cover Printer: Patterson Printing

Overcoming Math Anxiety

Copyright © 1993 by Randy Davidson and Ellen Levitov

Library of Congress Cataloging-in-Publication Data

Davidson, Randy.
     Overcoming math anxiety/Randy Davidson, Ellen Levitov.
        p.   cm.
     Includes index.
     ISBN 0-06-501651-3
     1. Math anxiety.   2. Mathematics—Study and teaching.   3. Self-help
techniques.   I. Levitov, Ellen.   II. Title.
QA11.D3465   1993
370.15'651—dc20   93-9485
                                                                        CIP

93 94 95 96 9 8 7 6 5 4 3 2 1

Contents

Preface

In the early 1980s, we were both employed at the University of New Orleans, Randy as a math instructor and Ellen as a counselor, when a mutual friend, Dennis Walsh, introduced us. It was the beginning of a long personal and working relationship.

We knew that many of our students experienced fear, frustration and failure in their math classes. Since we felt compelled to do something about this, we decided to team up and develop a workshop, using our combined skills and perspectives in helping our students. We held the first of our many "Overcoming Math Anxiety" workshops in 1983. They are presently conducted in two four-hour sessions, one week apart. They are attended by both university students and members of the community at large—some studying math and some not—men and women, young and old.

Because of the success of these workshops, we began to think about assisting a greater number of math anxious people. We decided to write this book, using a workbook format in hope of helping the readers to respond to our questions as they might in a workshop setting. Our approach is to have readers concentrate on reducing their anxiety so that they are able to learn and do math. Because readers will have a variety of mathematical backgrounds, some may find themselves unfamiliar with some examples. It is our hope that such readers will focus on the point of the method being presented as opposed to being caught up in the math itself.

And so we headed for a cabin in the Ozark Mountains for a week to begin work on this book. It was a beautiful setting in which to give birth to this book. We want to thank Tina Wilcox for letting us stay in her cabin. We worked by sunlight during the day and by kerosene lamps at night. From then on we worked on a regular basis, in between the demands of our jobs and major changes in both of our lives.

There have been many people who have given us great support through the years, and we thank them: David Shroyer for his constant support and his encouragement in starting the first "Overcoming Math Anxiety" workshop; David Skidmore for his assistance with relaxation techniques and many fantastic meals; Pat Thomas, for use of her cabin at the beach so that we could escape our hectic city lives to work more intensely; Fran Ricardo, for her enthusiasm and creative suggestions; our parents and siblings, for their constant encouragement; our husbands Mickey Lauria and Vern Baxter, for their support and assistance in using the computer; and our children: Michael, who was kind enough to come into this world two weeks late so that Randy could finish preparing the first draft of this book, and Kate, who gave up precious time with her mother while Ellen worked on preparing the book for publication.

There are still others to thank: Pat Connor and Justin Levitov, for their computer assistance; Paige Bennett, for her help in actually putting this book together; Susan Webre, for her wonderful artistic skills; John Hornsby, for his support from beginning to end; Chris Flug, for her proofreading; and, of course, our editor Anne Kelly and her assistant Lisa Kamins, who were always at the other end of the phone with answers to our questions.

Much devotion has gone into this book and we hope that you will get much out of it.

Randy Davidson

Ellen Levitov

Introduction

Are you intimidated by numbers? Do you "blank out" when you are asked to work an arithmetic problem? Have you been avoiding math courses? Do you find yourself saying, "I can't do math"? Was math your worst subject? Do you wonder why you do well in other subjects, but not math?

If you have these or any number of similar responses to math, you are one of many people who go through life suffering from math anxiety. Math anxiety is an emotional and physical response to math that hinders your ability to be successful mathematically. You become mathematically incapacitated. This is usually frustrating and embarrassing. No wonder you tend to avoid math situations! No wonder you might choose a college major because it has few mathematical requirements. You might even avoid pursuing a career just because the math requirement is too difficult.

Although you may want to hide from math, you really can't afford to. In this technological world, it plays a very important part in our everyday lives. Math is used when going to the grocery store, buying a car, checking bank statements, making investments, preparing taxes, making home improvements, and even baking cookies.

Your fear of math may also translate into a fear of technology. You are not alone. Many VCR owners are unable to set their equipment to tape a show when they are not home, or to even have their clocks set properly. This is the age of computers—from the cash register at the store, to airline reservations, to computers in your very own home. Your frustration may be compounded by the fact that your children could be computer wizards, while you wonder how to turn the darn thing on!

Some of you may aspire to become that computer wizard; some may want to be a better homemaker, or some of you may want to pass that math class. This book helps you achieve your math goals by assisting you in overcoming your math anxiety first.

The evolution of this book is a result of several years of conducting "Overcoming Math Anxiety" workshops at the University of New Orleans. We experienced much success with our math anxious students, and it is these students who inspired and supported the writing of this workbook. Throughout the book are echoes of our workshop participants' statements, concerns, expectations, fears, and successes. Typical participant responses are included in the exercises throughout the book under the heading OTHERS. They are there to help you recognize, as they did, that you are not alone in this quest.

The book is written in the form of a workbook, because math anxiety cannot be overcome by reading alone. Overcoming math anxiety requires active participation on your part. Working through the exercises in the sequence provided will take you through a process of self-discovery to help you understand why you experience math anxiety, and on to a series of tools that will help you in overcoming your math anxiety.

If you have taken the crucial step of enrolling in a math class, you are forced to confront math on a daily basis. You can practice dealing with your math anxiety using the tools you learn in this book, while in class or while doing your homework.

If you are not presently in a math class, you can practice with these tools when facing math in your daily life. Perhaps you will even feel strong enough to enroll in a math class at the next opportunity. In any case, working to overcome your math anxiety will help you to experience math in a more successful and positive way.

Finally, becoming math anxiety free means making changes in your life! Despite the fact that you have been experiencing math anxiety for so long that it seems you have had it since birth, there is no "math anxiety gene" that has been discovered. It is a *learned* behavior and can therefore be *unlearned*. Yet because the anxiety may have been with you for a long time, it would be unrealistic to expect that it could disappear quickly and easily. As you are probably aware, changes do not happen overnight or without hard work. Here's your opportunity to work hard and reap the rewards of **a life free of math anxiety!**

Part One

Self-Discovery

Chapter 1

Beginning Your Journey

Congratulations! In choosing this book, you have taken a very crucial first step to becoming free of math anxiety. You have decided to take action, to rid yourself once and for all of math anxious feelings—to no longer allow them to disable you!

In actuality, you are about to embark on a journey, a journey to becoming math anxiety free. This book will serve as your guide. You can expect this guidebook to provide you with information that will make your journey easier and more enjoyable. You will benefit from the experience of those who have traveled this road before you. On this journey, you will explore your math history; you will discover the best study techniques for math; you will learn to rest, reflect, and plan; and you will begin to feel the excitement of new success in math.

In planning a journey, you may experience a number of feelings simultaneously. Anticipation brings with it some fears, some excitement, some nervousness, and some expectations. In beginning to anticipate your journey to become math anxiety free, you are probably experiencing a number of emotions and expectations. Take a minute to think about your expectations.

What do you expect to gain from this book?

OTHERS:

I want to make the butterflies in my stomach disappear.

I want to learn to work fractions.

I want a miracle.

I want to stop panicking when I see a math test.

You may recognize some of these expectations as your own. What are you hoping to gain from reading and working through this book? Freely list your expectations below.

YOURS:

_____

_____

_____

_____

_____

_____

_____

You now have your list of expectations . . . Wouldn't it be wonderful for all of them to actually come true? The possibility for their being realized exists with your commitment to making them happen. In order to meet your expectations, and to have the best journey possible, certain preparations will be necessary.

An essential preparation for any journey is to gather appropriate equipment. Indeed, a ski mask would be inappropriate equipment for a cruise to the Bahamas! For your journey, the essential "equipment" will be your working space. Working at the kitchen table with your family moving about, the phone ringing, the television playing in the next room, and the dog barking is not a very conducive environment for concentration. A better environment consists of good lighting, a desk and chair, privacy, and quiet. Take a moment to choose your "equipment."

Where *do you plan to work on this book?*

OTHERS:

A desk in my bedroom

YOURS:

_____

_____

_____

When *do you plan to work on this book?*

OTHERS:

Every afternoon at 2 p.m., which is right when I get home from school

YOURS:

_____

_____

Another important preparation for the journey is the planning of your itinerary. Sit back and relax, because the best possible route has already been mapped out for you. Our experience has led us to develop a process by which you move from having math anxious feelings to becoming math anxiety free. This process begins with an exploration of your past and present experiences concerning math. It is an essential starting place. It will provide you with a way of understanding your anxiety that will allow you to fully utilize the subsequent techniques for overcoming it. As you work through the structured set of exercises in this book, you will be practicing these techniques, reinforcing the new ideas and gaining confidence. So, in your journey, simply work the exercises from beginning to end in the order presented. It will be at your own expense should you decide to skip around!

With your "equipment" and "itinerary" in hand, you are ready to embark on your journey. As your tour guides, we would like to give you some last minute send-off suggestions. First, be an *active* tourist! In using this book to the fullest, you should do all of the exercises. In doing them, be honest with yourself—write comments in the margins and be involved as much as possible.

Second, take care of yourself! Some exercises that you will encounter are difficult because they require some introspection. Allow yourself the time necessary to get in touch with the information sought in the exercise. Remember to pat yourself on the back for the work you are doing, and reward yourself frequently.

What are the ways you plan to reward yourself?

OTHERS:
taking a hot bubble bath
eating a hot fudge sundae
taking a bicycle ride

YOURS:
_____
_____
_____
_____
_____

Be sure to reward yourself *often*.

You're now ready. Have a successful journey to becoming math anxiety free.
BON VOYAGE!

Chapter 2

Exploring Symptoms

MATH ANXIETY . . . Is your knee-jerk reaction to the mention of these two little words, "That's what I've got!"? If so, even the thought of having to perform math may trigger fear, avoidance, or panic.

You probably feel quite sure that you are the only one who experiences such anxiety. You may also feel sure that everyone notices your difficulty with math. It should help you to know that in reality you are not alone. (As a matter of fact, we would not sell any books if you were!)

In our workshop, we find that participants have an overwhelming sense of relief when they discover that other people experience math anxiety. When one participant discloses his or her own math anxious feelings, others often respond by nodding and making comments such as, "Yeah, that's exactly what happens to me!!!" They are amazed to hear that others' anxiety is even more acute than their own. Perhaps people you know also have math anxiety, even though they may have been keeping it a secret. If you so desire, ask some of your fellow students or friends if they experience math anxiety. You'll probably discover that you are definitely not alone!

If someone were to ask you, "How do you *know* that you have math anxiety?" what would you say? You might very well respond by mentioning some of the ways in which you experience math anxiety. We call such experiences *symptoms* of math anxiety.

What symptoms do you experience?

OTHERS:

sweaty palms

a racing heart

feeling panicked

my mind goes blank

Everyone experiences a different set of symptoms.

Take a moment to name your symptoms.

YOURS:

_____

_____

_____

_____

_____

Perhaps there are other symptoms of math anxiety that you experience but forgot to list because you are not presently feeling anxious. In order to help you remember all of your symptoms, take the following quiz. Envision this quiz as if it is a test to be graded. Imagine yourself in a math class taking a timed exam. You may use a calculator, but it is not necessary. You have 10 minutes. Time yourself!

Quiz: Time 10 Minutes

1. Compute 12% of 85.

2. Subract the following fractions.

$$\frac{2}{3} - \frac{1}{2} =$$

3. A rectangular yard has a length which is twice its width. The perimeter of the yard is 150 feet. What is the area of the yard?

4. Solve for x.

$$2(x - 3) = -12$$

5. Using each of the digits from 1 to 9 exactly once, place the digits in the square so that the total of each row, column, and each of the main diagonals is 15.

STOP!

10

What have you been experiencing since you were asked to take the quiz?

OTHERS:

My palms got sweaty.

I kept thinking, "I should know how to do this."

My mind went blank.

I thought, "I got the answer, but I did it the wrong way."

My stomach felt uneasy.

I thought, "Oh no, I can't remember the formula."

I thought, "Obviously, I just can't do math!"

I thought, "They've got to be kidding. I thought this was supposed to help.

I want a refund!"

YOURS:

_____

_____

_____

_____

_____

_____

(Answers to the quiz are in Appendix A.)

Compare your responses with the list you made prior to the quiz. Did you experience the same symptoms? Did you discover some symptoms that you had forgotten to mention or that you had been unaware of before?

At this point, some of you might be thinking, "Oh my gosh, look at these new symptoms that I've acquired! I already had plenty! I must be more anxious than I thought!" Don't worry—these are not new symptoms, only symptoms you had in the past without being totally aware of them. By concentrating on your reactions as you took the quiz, you simply became more aware of your own responses.

And that's good! Your math anxious symptoms are to be welcomed! They serve as a distress signal. Like a flashing red light, they call your attention to the fact that you are currently experiencing math anxiety. If these symptoms are occurring without your realizing it, you cannot pinpoint your anxiety or its source. Only once you are able to name these symptoms will you be able to effectively work on controlling your math anxiety. The more aware you become, the more opportunity you have to combat the problem.

Recognizing that your hands are sweaty encourages you to ask yourself, "What's going on?" With that question, you automatically become focused on your symptom. For many, merely being conscious of the symptoms will be enough to reduce or stop the anxious feelings. The time you take to focus on the symptom is a resting point. It allows you to assess your situation and to make a choice—continue the anxiety, reduce it, or stop it. All of this may happen very quickly, perhaps in a split second, but you still have the chance to stop that escalating feeling of becoming more and more anxious.

Are you sitting and thinking, "Do you mean to tell me that I can choose to have this anxiety or I can choose *not* to have it?" Though it may be difficult to accept at this time, we are saying just that! However, we are not saying that this choice is a simple one. With practice in recognizing and naming your symptoms, combined with the tools that you will learn in Part Two, you will find yourself more ready and able to make such choices.

At this point, let's practice recognizing and naming math anxious symptoms. Work on the following math problems, but stop to record your math anxious symptoms whenever they occur. You may experience anxiety as soon as you see the first problem or perhaps not until the last problem. Try to work the problems that you feel would make you the most anxious. As soon as you begin to experience some anxiety, record the symptoms on the lines next to the problem on which you are working. Keep in mind that our emphasis is on the feelings you're having as you work the problems and not so much on working the problems correctly.

PROBLEMS	SYMPTOMS

1. Subtract.

   5.017 - 3.94 =

2. Simplify.

$$\frac{3 \ (7 \ - \ 9) \ - \ 10}{5 \ (3 \ - \ 4) \ + \ 1}$$

3. Find the area of a triangle with a base 10 centimeters and height 4 centimeters.

4. Jane is one year older than her brother Bill. Their father is three times as old as Bill. If the sum of Jane's, Bill's, and their father's ages is 76, find each of their ages.

5. Simplify completely.

$$\sqrt{6} + \sqrt{12} + \sqrt{24} + \sqrt{27}$$

6. Add.

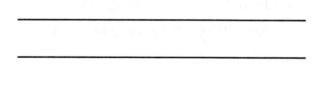

$$\frac{3}{x + 1} + \frac{x}{x^2 + 2x + 1}$$

(Answers to this problem set are in Appendix B.)

You have now had some practice recognizing and naming your symptoms. Were you aware that your anxious feelings momentarily stopped as you concentrated on the symptoms you were experiencing? Maybe you were even lucky enough to also experience some reduction in your overall level of anxiety! (If not, don't worry because it is only important that you learn to recognize and name your symptoms at this stage.) The more you consciously practice naming your symptoms, the smoother the transition will be to the next step in the process, which is making the choice to lessen your anxiety.

In working these problems, were there any problems that were not anxiety-provoking for you? If yes, you obviously have and are already using methods to prevent anxious feelings from occurring in some cases. It is important to become aware of these nonanxious times. If you recognize that you can do some math in a nonanxious state, you can become aware of those methods that help you and then apply them to other situations. You may have felt comfortable with a certain problem because you had worked that type in the past and felt familiar with it, or because you said to yourself, "I'm not worried about this, because it is not a real test!"

What was it that helped you avoid anxious feelings in working those problems?

_____

_____

_____

_____

Whatever your reasoning or method of approach, it is something you can learn to utilize when solving anxiety-provoking problems in the future. You can continue to concentrate on being aware of your math anxious symptoms as you carry on in your daily life.

For practice, write about a math anxious situation you have experienced in the past and answer the following questions.

OTHERS:

SITUATION: I was in charge of figuring out how much food was needed for the party after a triathlon. I was afraid someone would ask me how much food was needed before I had the time to sit down and figure it out.

THEIR SYMPTOMS
OF ANXIETY: shaky, sweaty, tight stomach; and thinking "I won't be able to figure this out quickly enough!"

ACTION THEY TOOK: I told myself that if someone asked, I could tell them that I hadn't figured it out yet and that I would let them know when I had. Then, I did the work as quickly as I could with a calculator.

THEY LEARNED
THAT: I am too worried about what others will think.

YOURS:

SITUATION:

_____

_____

_____

_____

_____

_____

_____

_____

_____

YOUR SYMPTOMS OF ANXIETY:

_____

_____

_____

_____

_____

WHAT ACTION DID YOU TAKE?

_____

_____

_____

_____

_____

_____

I LEARNED THAT:

_____

_____

_____

_____

_____

Take a break from reading the book and spend the next few days becoming aware of your anxiety symptoms as they appear in math-related situations. Record your experiences in the math journal in Appendix C.

Congratulations! You have now begun your own personal math journal. Feel free to write in it whenever you want to.

By now, through your practice, you should be keenly aware of your symptoms almost immediately upon their occurrence. Stay alert as you continue to work through your anxiety. In completing the work in this chapter, you have begun the process of becoming math anxiety free by recognizing and naming your symptoms.

Chapter 3

Origins

"When I was in fourth grade, the teacher asked me to work a problem at
the board. I couldn't work it. I stood there awhile, totally embarrassed.
Eventually, the teacher came to the blackboard, asked me to sit down, and
showed the class how to work the problem. I was so embarrassed. That
was when I knew that I obviously couldn't do math."

The adult in the above example generalized his inability to work a single arithmetic
problem at the board in the fourth grade to his inability to perform math in general.
Today, he experiences math anxiety.

Perhaps you can recall a similar experience that contributes to your feelings about math.
This may be one of many experiences that fostered your math anxiety. It is natural for
math anxious people to wonder how they got that way. In this chapter you will broaden
your understanding by looking more closely at your past experiences, messages from
society, messages from school, and messages from significant people.

PAST EXPERIENCES

Our workshop participants have little difficulty when asked to recall an incident from their
past that influenced their present feelings about math. One of these stories follows.

"My dad's always been a whiz in math. He's an engineer. When I would ask him for help with my math homework, he would try to help for a few minutes. But he got frustrated with me and left when I couldn't understand. He said that I should catch on much faster and that made me feel dumb. I knew then that I would never be able to live up to his expectations, even though I keep trying."

This adult experiences math anxiety because of early experiences with his father.

As you can see, parents as well as teachers, strongly influence our mathematical self-concept by what they tell us and how they act. Perhaps a mother feels that she is unable to help her child with math homework. She may tell her child to "Ask your father" or "It's too difficult for me. I can't do this new math." What does her child learn? Her child may interpret this to mean that the material is difficult and may wonder, "Gee, how will I ever understand this, if even Mom can't?" Another interpretation is that "girls don't need to know how to do math since mom doesn't know it."

What have you learned about math and your mathematical ability? Where and how did you learn it? You can begin to answer these questions by doing the following exercise.

Describe in detail one experience from your past that is particularly memorable and influential in your attitudes about math. Where were you? How old were you ? Who was there? What was said? What did you do? How did you feel?

____

____

____

____

____

____

____

_____

_____

_____

_____

_____

_____

Continue to search into your past by completing the following math history.

MATH HISTORY

1. *Describe and draw a picture of your least favorite math teacher.*

2. *Describe your favorite math teacher.*

_____

_____

_____

_____

_____

3. *Describe your present math teacher, if you have one. (Draw a picture, if you like.)*

4. *Describe when you first experienced difficulties in math.*

_____

_____

_____

_____

_____

_____

5. *Describe when you first stopped liking math.*

_____

_____

_____

_____

_____

_____

6. *How did your father feel about math? And how does that affect your feelings about math?*

_____

_____

_____

_____

_____

7. *How did your mother feel about math? And how does that affect your feelings about math?*

_____

_____

_____

_____

_____

_____

_____

8. *How did your brother(s) and/or sister(s) feel about math? And how does that affect your feelings about math?*

_____

_____

_____

_____

_____

_____

_____

_____

9. *Draw and describe the "math whiz kid."*

10. *Describe your ability to do math.*

_____

_____

_____

_____

_____

_____

11. *How do you feel when you do math?*

_____

_____

_____

_____

_____

_____

12. *List everything that comes to mind in completing this statement: Math is . . .*

_____

_____

_____

_____

_____

_____

_____

The time that you have just spent on your math history should be helpful in your investigation of the origins of your math anxiety. Was there a particular math teacher who embarrassed you in class? Were your mother and father giving you messages that you didn't need to know math? Maybe your parents had a separation which disturbed you while you were in third grade, and soon after you began to experience difficulties in math. It is extremely beneficial to discover when and why you first began to experience difficulties with math.

One of our early workshop participants told an interesting story as part of her math history, in which personal difficulties interfered with her math studies. This woman was interested in an arts-oriented education, but her parents forced her to go to a scientifically oriented high school. She was obviously unhappy about the school and unfortunately brought her resentment with her to her first class of the day—math. She was unable or unwilling to give math the attention it needed at that time. Interestingly, this woman had not experienced math anxiety prior to this time; in fact, she did not have any major problems with the subject. It was only once she became upset at having to study math at the "wrong school" that she "got behind" in her math studies and began experiencing some anxiety.

As this woman's story illustrates, childhood experiences can have a lasting affect. Divorce of parents, a move to a new city, or a change in schools are all disruptive. In the midst of such turmoil, a child may neglect schoolwork or may be unable to concentrate. Then, when they "miss" some math concepts, it is easy to fall behind and difficult to catch up. Subsequently, it becomes more difficult to learn new material because they do not understand the concepts on which the new material is based. Math anxiety easily develops when a child feels that he or she is "hopelessly behind." A vicious cycle begins as the anxiety makes it difficult to learn math, and the difficulties with math in turn perpetuate the anxiety.

As in the case of the child who has fallen behind in math because of unrelated emotional problems, a child may also fall behind because of unmatched learning and teaching styles. Those of you whose teachers used methods best suited to your own rate and style of learning are fortunate; however, in the teacher's attempt to reach the "normal" or "average" student, the rest of us have either been left behind or bored. If as a child you had difficulty understanding a particular concept, or needed more time to assimilate an already understood concept, you may have fallen behind the teacher's "average" pace. Once again, falling behind can put a child into an anxiety cycle.

The point here is that you may have become caught up in an anxiety cycle quite possibly for reasons *not having to do with your innate math ability*! In fact, you may be able to recall a time in your life when you thought of yourself as "good in math" (or at least not bad at it!)—a time when you were able to handle math concepts appropriate to your age, without experiencing math anxiety.

Try it. Think back to a time in your life when you did __not__ experience math anxiety. This may be many years ago, going back to your early childhood. If you can, describe that time when you were not anxious about math. How old were you? How did you feel about math? If you cannot recall right away, take a break and think about it for awhile.

_____

_____

_____

_____

_____

_____

_____

If you were able to do the exercise, it may be a real eye-opener to discover that you once felt more positive about math than you do now, and that you were not having major difficulties with the subject. That's because you were capable of doing math then and you still are! Math anxiety is *not* a problem of intelligence. It is a learned behavior that can be unlearned.

MESSAGES FROM SOCIETY

Societal messages reflect our society's attitudes and beliefs about math and mathematicians. They permeate our culture and are passed on to people through television, books, teachers and parents. Those messages about math can greatly influence you and contribute to your math anxiety, in spite of your math skills.

The most prevalent societal message is that "math is for men." Traditional role models always include men engaged in scientific work involving math, and women involved in a helping profession requiring little math. Parents and teachers often will guide children toward an "appropriate" field. Because of these expectations, many girls learn that it's o.k. to give up when they don't understand something, because "girls don't need to know math."

Another message tells us that a certain type of person is good in math. We seem to classify people into those who "can" and those who "cannot" do math. We say that those who "can" do math have a "math mind." Our stereotypical image of the math wizard or math professor accentuates this division of the population. He is a socially inept male with glasses (and pimples in his youth) referred to as "the brain." His pockets are filled with an assortment of pencils and a calculator. Does your picture of the "math whiz kid" in question #9 of your Math History fit this description?

Often, a math anxious individual has taken these messages quite literally. Thus, if she or he does not fit the stereotype, it follows that she or he is "not good in math." The truth is that both men and women have a full range of mathematical ability. Things are not simply a matter of gender.

MESSAGES FROM SCHOOL

Many of society's messages treat math in a special way. In many cases, these messages are transmitted through our educational system. Let's look at some of these messages and examine them critically.

"To be good at math, I have to be fast."

As students we get the impression that speed is very important. After all, we are expected to assimilate totally new concepts after a single lecture; we must take tests within a prescribed amount of time and, perhaps most dramatically of all, we watch our teachers work problems much more quickly than we can. Yet we seldom give much thought to the fact that teachers can work quickly because they have already gone through the learning process and have had a great deal of practice working those problems. Have you ever realized that if your teacher were to approach a new concept, she would have to struggle through the same learning process you do by studying, practicing, questioning and thinking? It would take time for her to work those new problems.

One develops speed at working problems by practicing, not by working specifically on speed. As in practicing a musical instrument or a movement in sports, repetition at a comfortable rate trains your mind and body so that the skill becomes automatic. Eventually, you can work with both ease and speed.

Within the context of a classroom situation, when one is asked to take a timed exam, one often begins to worry "I don't work fast enough!" Once you have had enough practice, then working the problems will have become automatic and, in fact, you *will* work them more quickly.

"I should be able to do the work in my head!"

It is impressive when people can compute a series of calculations in their heads, and get the right answer as well. Such ability, as we say in New Orleans, is "lagniappe," or something extra. It is perfectly acceptable and quite indeed normal to use paper or a calculator. The use of such aids increases the chance of being accurate. For most of us, the small amount of time saved by working in our head is rarely worth the error likely to be made. Advantages to written work are that you or someone else can follow your thinking process step by step, and find errors that might have occurred in your calculations or logic. We can admire those who have the talent of working in their heads, yet we need to realize that such talent is not a prerequisite for being able to do math.

"I didn't get the right answer, so I must not know what I'm doing!"

How important is accuracy? When we make errors while working a problem, we will subsequently get the wrong answer. It could be a crucial mistake in certain situations: building a bridge and dispensing medications require a great deal of accuracy. On the other hand, when we are in the midst of *learning* a mathematical concept or process, the importance of accuracy is reduced. An arithmetic error that causes you to get the wrong answer is not so bad if you understand the process. Whether or not you always get the right answers, give yourself credit for going through the procedure correctly because that is the difficult part. Of course, while taking a test, you want to maximize your accuracy. If you remember not to work too fast or do too much in your head, you can increase accuracy. If your mistake is only arithmetic, some teachers reward you for showing that you understand the process by giving partial credit.

"I got the right answer, but I did it the wrong way," or " I got the answer, but I don't know how."

These statements imply that there is *only one way* to solve a problem. Often only one method is taught. It is usually the most widely accepted and used method.

But you may come up with an alternative method of solving a problem. Or you may mysteriously come up with the answer without realizing exactly how. Rather than seeing this negatively, pat yourself on the back for being creative and intuitive, and try to analyze your alternative method. You may find that your method is very closely related to the one presented. If not, it is useful to compare the two methods and discuss why one might be more useful than the other. In a class situation, the class method is easier to use (though not necessarily better), because it will facilitate communication while discussing the problems.

If you do not know how you got the answer to a problem, it may take some effort to figure out what it was that your mind did. Again, this is not bad. *Do* recognize that you figured out the answer and *that* in itself deserves credit! Then examine your thinking. It will be very rewarding to discover your own thought processes. Once you decipher them, you can apply them to similar problems. And you can feel proud!

"I'm a language person. I'm not good in math and science!"

"Language people" believe that their struggles with math are due to a lack of ability, and that the relative ease they feel when they work in other areas signifies a natural talent in those areas. Of course, once we label ourselves in such a way, our expectations are affected. You work harder in your better courses and give up more easily in your weaker areas. This labeling only serves to diminish your ability to really succeed in math.

The language of nonscientific courses is English. Such courses involve reading and writing. Since our exposure to English begins at birth, we have a head start in understanding our language before we must learn its symbols and grammatical rules in school. We have some but not nearly as much preparation in math. When we learn math in school, it seems to be nothing more than a bunch of rules, formulas and symbols without meaning. This can make us feel strange. To combat this alienating image, it may help to look at the fact that English and math are both built on symbols and rules. Math is a language, too. In fact, it is the universal language that scientists use to model our world.

"Math uses logic, not intuition"

Not only is math seen as foreign, it is also labeled as being purely logical. Creative and intuitive people often feel distant from such a logical discipline. But creativity and intuition do play a role in mathematics.

When solving a problem, try taking a break from actively working on the problem. During this rest period, your mind will process the information and put pieces of the puzzle together. Have you ever suddenly felt that burst of mental energy that can only be phrased, "Ah ha, I know what to do!" It can happen while doing something unrelated like exercise, housework, play, or sleep. Your insight helps you proceed with the solution. Of course, once you have discovered the solution to a problem, you will want to write it down, logically, so that others can read and follow your work.

Isn't this similar to the creative process in other fields? Creative ideas or work in other fields must also be organized in some (logical) way so as to present it to other people. Isn't that what we do when we write an essay? We first think about the topic, then write down a *logical* outline, then we proceed with writing the essay. All of these steps are followed in order so that when someone reads our essay, it is concise and clear, as well as logical. The same holds true for math.

MESSAGES FROM SIGNIFICANT PEOPLE

As we said earlier, there are many messages transmitted in our society that pertain to mathematics, to mathematicians, and to those learning math. Imagine these messages displayed on a banner floating around in the sky. If we did not pay attention to them, they would not affect us. Unfortunately, we do tend to read the banners. The problem is that these messages are not only passed on by society at large, but also by important people in our lives—parents, teachers, and friends. We tend to believe these people, accept what they say, and value their opinions.

Parents and teachers (usually unknowingly) emphasize or reinforce societal values and beliefs. We are most susceptible to their opinions. While parents or teachers often reinforce male/female role models and other societal messages, they may also create messages of their own. For instance, a parent may say, "Mary has always been better in math than Sue." Sue grows up thinking her math abilities are inadequate or lower than they should be, though both children may have great math potential. As another example, a teacher may say, "You should know that already," or "This is easy." As a result, a student may feel inadequate, despite the fact that she is capable of learning the material.

These messages from our parents and teachers may trigger our feelings of math anxiety. Because consciously or unconsciously we want to "match" the expectations people who are important to us have for us, we tend to place a greatly exaggerated sense of importance on our math performance. With such high stakes, it is easy to understand why one might develop math anxiety.

CONCLUSION

In this chapter, you have been searching for the origins of your math anxiety. You have looked at your past experiences, the messages you have received from society, and the messages given to you by significant people in your life. As a result, there are messages that you have internalized. These messages you now carry with you.

33

List below all of those messages that you are now carrying. Also try to assess the origin of each of these messages.

OTHERS:

Messages

1. "I'm too slow."
2. "I'm a woman, so I should be a teacher, not an engineer."

Where message comes from

1. sixth grade teacher
2. society

YOURS:

Messages

Where message comes from

_____

_____

_____

_____

_____

_____

_____

In looking over your list of messages, you may realize that they came from outside of you and you internalized them. Since these are learned messages, they can be UNLEARNED! Part Two of this book will help you unlearn these messages and create new ones.

Part Two

Tools for Overcoming Math Anxiety

You have reached a resting point on your journey to becoming free of math anxiety—time to relax for a moment to assess your progress and to look forward to your next step.

In Part One, you completed a necessary part of your journey in which you experienced and examined your symptoms of math anxiety and their origins. Perhaps you have already begun to notice a movement away from being math anxious. In Part Two, you begin the next leg of your journey, by learning and practicing specific techniques designed to help you become free of math anxiety.

As a math anxious person, you probably experience a lack of confidence in your math ability. Because of this lack of confidence, you approach mathematics differently than someone who is confident in his or her math ability. When a math anxious person begins working a math problem, he fears he will not be able to complete it correctly. If a math anxious person is "stuck" in working a problem, he will give up in exasperation and use this failure to justify his own feelings of incompetence. On the other hand, when a math anxious person successfully completes a math problem, he will self-critically assume that the "problem is an easy one" or that "I just got lucky." A math anxious person is unable to recognize his own success when it does occur.

As you proceed with the second leg of your journey, the tools you learn will bring you closer to being a math confident person. As that happens, you will feel increasingly sure of yourself whenever you approach a math problem. You will still get "stuck," but when this happens, you will likely react by stopping and *calmly* reassessing your work. You might also react by taking a break for awhile and allowing your intuition to work. Even if you do give up on the problem, your attitude is more likely to be "Oh, well . . ." than "Gosh, am I stupid." Rather than seeing this as a failure, you will recognize that you have moments of weakness as well as strength; that sometimes you are more able to focus on the problem than at other times; and that some problems may be more difficult for you than others. When you do complete a math problem successfully as a math confident person, you will accept the success and use it to further build your confidence.

Your goal is to gain an attitude more like the math confident person. That's the final destination of this journey.

Chapter 4

Using the Inner Voice

This chapter discusses the first of five techniques to overcoming math anxiety—using the inner voice. Though you may be completely unaware of your inner voice, it can affect you in both negative and positive ways. On the negative side, your inner voice is a major contributing factor to both causing and promoting your math anxiety. On the positive side, you can learn to utilize it to help in overcoming your math anxiety. This will be accomplished by examining the following questions: What is the inner voice? How does it affect you? How can you take control of your inner voice?

To answer the first question, "What is your inner voice?" imagine a typical Monday morning with the alarm clock ringing at 6 a.m. You turn over in bed, put the pillow over your head, and say to yourself, "I'll sleep just another few minutes." As you begin to doze off, another thought comes to mind, "I had better get up and get moving." Then you hear yet another idea, "If I skip breakfast, I can sleep just a little bit longer."

Most of the action in this Monday morning scenario takes place solely within your head. You are actually holding an internal discussion conducted by your inner voice. It is the voice that speaks to you, giving you messages that no one else can hear. As you become aware of your inner voice, you will discover that it is very active. Sometimes it is loud and tells you exactly what to do. Other times it asks questions, and often it gives you answers.

Now that you are aware of your inner voice, you will probably find yourself hearing it more and more. The more you consciously listen for it, the greater awareness you will have of your inner voice. Increased awareness will help you recognize how your inner voice influences your reactions. For example, telling yourself, "I know that I can do it!" helps you react confidently, whereas your confidence is easily eroded by hearing the thought, "I've never been good at this."

In particular, your inner voice plays an important role in influencing your reactions to math-related situations. To illustrate this point, let us look at a common setting involving some arithmetic. Suppose that you have just completed a meal at a restaurant with five other people. When the waiter arrives with the bill, *you* are the one given the task of figuring out how much money each person owes. Your inner voice immediately goes to work. "I don't know why they gave the bill to me. I've never been able to do this. Last time I did it, I ended up paying five dollars extra. I obviously can't do it correctly. What is everybody going to think?" You probably feel panic-stricken as you begin to work at equitably dividing the bill. Your inner voice continues, "Why can't I do this simple arithmetic? Everybody is waiting for me and I just can't do it!" With such thoughts, or messages, you ultimately miscalculate or you simply give up and pass the bill on to someone else.

In this restaurant scene, the messages that you gave yourself helped to create and maintain your anxiety. Your anxiety then caused you to fail at this math-related task. In reality you have become entangled in a vicious cycle. The presentation of the bill immediately invoked negative inner messages. It was in response to these negative messages that you began to feel anxious. This anxiety gave birth to more negative messages which in turn prevented you from successfully working at dividing the bill. Because of this unsuccessful experience, you will continue to give yourself negative inner messages, which will in turn cause you to be fearful of experiencing a similar situation in the future. When confronted with the situation again, you will once more find the cycle repeating itself. (See Figure 1.)

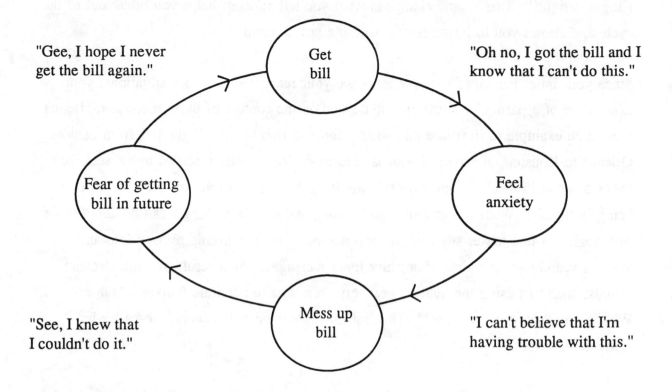

"Gee, I hope I never get the bill again."

Get bill

"Oh no, I got the bill and I know that I can't do this."

Fear of getting bill in future

Feel anxiety

"See, I knew that I couldn't do it."

Mess up bill

"I can't believe that I'm having trouble with this."

Figure 1. The anxiety cycle: restaurant bill.

Once hooked into this cycle, you begin to feel *powerless*. It feels as if someone is taking you around and around on an amusement ride that you cannot get off or stop. You continue around the same circular path over and over again, not knowing where it began or where it will end.

Once you realize that you are indeed hooked into such a cycle, it is natural to ask if it is possible to break out of it. *How* can you break out of this cycle? *How* can you regain your power? The answer lies in the fact that the "someone" who is taking you on the ride is yourself. Those negative inner messages that you give yourself are what push you along from one stage to the next. So, in order to break out of this cycle you need only stop giving yourself those negative messages. You can do this by changing those negative inner messages into positive ones. *Any* of the messages that perpetuate this cycle can be changed. For instance, the negative message given in the diagram, "I can't believe that I'm having trouble with this" could be countered by saying, "Gee, this isn't working out.

41

I'll have to rework it. Everyone can wait. There is no rush. If I take my time, I'm sure I'll get it right." This simple change in what you tell yourself helps you break out of the cycle and allows you to be successful with the task at hand.

Since your inner messages strongly influence your reactions to certain situations, your experience of a particular situation will depend on the content of those messages. Let us look at an example to illustrate this point. Suppose Bob boards Flight 101 from New Orleans to Houston on a typical Monday morning. After getting settled in his seat, he looks down at his seatbelt and says to himself, "I hope this is over quickly. I can't stand being in the air. What if something goes wrong and there's nothing I can do about it?" Bob begins to feel tense, sweaty, hot, and nervous. He is working himself into an anxious state by giving himself negative inner messages. As a result, routine airplane sounds, such as raising the landing gear, give him fuel to continue thinking, "Oh no! What's wrong with the engine?" This last inner message only serves to escalate his anxious responses.

Let's replay this scene differently. This time suppose that after buckling his seatbelt, Bob says to himself, "I really hate flying and I'm a bit nervous, but I do this every Monday and there's never been a problem before. I'm sure that the flight will go fine." At this point, Bob is able to take his mind off the flight and calmly read the morning paper. After takeoff, he hears the landing gear lifting and says to himself, "Oh no! What's that noise? Oh I remember, they're just raising the landing gear. Breakfast should be coming around soon." Though still somewhat on guard, Bob is neither sweaty, hot, nor tense. He has successfully calmed himself by using positive inner messages.

It is obvious that Bob's experience on the flight depends on which messages he chooses to give himself. In the first case, he made himself tense and anxious, while in the second case, he was able to relax. Bob had a choice of which message to give himself. Having this choice implies that Bob is in control of what he thinks and is therefore in control of his reactions. He has created his own experience.

You, too, have a choice in what messages you give yourself. You, too, are in control of what you think and how you react to life situations. The following exercise will help you pinpoint your own math-related inner messages and will help you understand why you give yourself those messages. You will then be asked to create positive inner messages so that you will in turn have more positive math-related experiences.

Look back to the exercises on pages 11, 13, and 14 in which you listed your reactions to the math sets. Some of your reactions are inner messages. List those inner messages below. Feel free to include other inner messages that you give yourself concerning math. As we have modeled, write inner messages as if you were speaking, using quotation marks.

OTHERS:

"I should know how to do this."

"I got the answer, but I did it the wrong way."

"On no! I can't remember the formula."

"Obviously, I just can't do math!"

"They've got to be kidding. I thought this book was supposed to help! I want a refund!"

YOURS:

_____

_____

_____

_____

_____

_____

_____

Look over your list and place an "N" in front of those inner messages that are negative and a "P" in front of those that are positive. <u>All</u> of our examples are negative inner messages.

Continue by doing the following.

1. *Choose one negative inner messages from your list—one that you "hear" most often. Write it in the space provided.*

OTHERS:
Obviously I just can't do math!

YOURS:
_____

2. *Write down all of the <u>disadvantages</u> of giving yourself this negative inner message.*

OTHERS:
Saying, "I just can't do math!" makes me feel like giving up. It makes me feel defeated. I feel like I'll never be able to do math. I lose my sense of self-worth. It makes me begin to doubt that I'll ever be able to be a nurse.

YOURS:
_____

_____

_____

_____

_____

_____

_____

3. *Rewrite your negative inner message as a positive one.*

OTHERS:
 I *can* do math!

YOURS:

_____

4. *What <u>keeps you</u> from using this positive inner message?*

OTHERS:

People will expect me to keep doing well in math.

I may reach my goal and that scares me.

I'll have to put in the time and effort in order to accomplish my goal.

I'll have to accept full responsibility for myself and not depend on others to help me.

I won't have an excuse for not becoming a nurse.

(Note: This question may be difficult to answer because it involves recognition of some things we may not like in ourselves. If we can discover and accept these things, we will be in a better position to stop avoiding and begin using positive inner messages.)

YOURS:

_____

_____

_____

_____

_____

_____

5. *Write down all the <u>advantages</u> of giving yourself this positive inner message.*

OTHERS:

I'll stay with the problem longer and hopefully get it right.

I will feel good about myself. I will feel energetic.

I feel like I could do anything!

I feel more optimistic about reaching my goals.

I feel more independent.

YOURS:

_____

_____

_____

_____

_____

_____

PROCESSING THE EXERCISE

Take a few minutes to look back over the exercise. You were asked to state a negative message, look at its disadvantages, assess why you continue to use it, change it to a positive statement, and realize the advantages of using this positive inner message. This exercise may have invoked many different feelings and emotions for you.

Try to write down any feelings that you may have had.

OTHERS:

In working through this exercise, I felt a variety of emotions, ending with a sense of "freeing up." When I noticed my own fears and insecurities, I felt disappointed in myself. It was unpleasant to recognize that I was "scared to reach my goal," but it took identifying these feelings to enable me to begin changing my negative inner message to a positive one. The advantages of giving myself the positive inner message further helped me to free myself of draining feelings. Hence, I ended the exercise feeling lighter, excited, and re-energized.

YOURS:

_____

_____

_____

_____

_____

_____

_____

_____

_____

Take your positive inner message and incorporate it into your life. **Use it!** At first it may feel awkward, as it might when trying on some new clothes that are not your usual style. Even though you give yourself this new positive message, you may not fully believe that it is true. The more you persist in using your positive inner message, the more comfortable you will become with it; just as through wearing it, you can become more comfortable with a new style of clothing. The more familiar your positive inner message becomes, the easier it will be to believe; soon the new look simply becomes your look. So use your positive inner message over and over again to really make it yours!

To complete the exercise, take each negative message listed on page 45 and rewrite a positive one. Any positive messages that you had listed already should be included here as well, since they are good messages to continue to give yourself.

OTHERS:

 I can figure this one out.

Although I got the answer in a different way, I'm proud of my own inventiveness.

I won't worry; I know the formula will come to me.

I can do math!

There must be a good reason for doing this quiz. I'll try it and see what happens.

YOURS:

_____

_____

_____

_____

_____

_____

_____

Now you should have a whole list of *positive* inner messages, a tool to help you break out of the anxiety cycle. With these positive inner messages you are on the road to creating more positive experiences. Remember, they are only helpful when used!

CONCLUSION

Math anxiety-provoking situations, like the scene in the restaurant, are likely to occur in your daily life, particularly if you are currently in a math class. You can practice becoming aware of your inner voice and changing negative messages to positive ones as these situations arise. (See Appendix D.)

When you have experienced your next math anxiety provoking situation, do the following exercise.

1. <u>*Describe*</u> *the situation in which you were feeling anxious and were aware of your inner voice at work.*

_____

_____

_____

_____

_____

_____

_____

_____

_____

_____

2. **_List_** *the inner messages that you gave yourself, both negative and positive.*

_____

_____

_____

_____

_____

_____

_____

3. **_Describe_** *your feelings and experiences that resulted from these inner messages.*

_____

_____

_____

_____

_____

_____

_____

4. *If you changed a negative inner message to a positive one, __state__ both the old and the new messages and then __describe__ how the change affected your experience.*

_____

_____

_____

_____

_____

_____

_____

You may have more anxiety-provoking situations than this exercise will accommodate. If so, there is a journal entry in Appendix E for your use.

We hope that you are becoming more aware of your inner messages—automatically changing the negative ones to positive ones, and feeling less and less anxious in such situations. Be sure to use those positive inner messages as often as possible and make them a part of you.

Chapter 5

Relaxaaaaaaaation

This chapter is devoted to learning the technique of relaxation—the second tool for overcoming math anxiety. Relaxation usually occurs right before dropping off to sleep, during a hot bath, or during a long massage. When you become very deeply relaxed, your body enters a different state, called an alpha state. Your whole body becomes calm: your heartbeat slows down, your muscles release tension, and your breathing becomes regular. The Relaxation Technique is a method for bringing yourself to this desired state of relaxation at the moment of your choosing. Relaxation enables you to return to your work calm and refreshed, more focused, and with more clarity.

How can relaxation help you in overcoming your math anxiety? In Chapter 2, you named physical reactions that you experience when confronted by mathematics, such as sweating, increased heartrate, and/or muscle tension. You can learn to control these physical symptoms by relaxing, to lessen their effect on your math performance. Additionally, as we discussed in the last chapter, you react to mathematical stimulants by giving yourself certain negative messages. You have re-examined your negative messages and in turn created positive ones. You can use relaxation to reinforce positive messages by saying them to yourself while in a relaxed state. As you become more familiar with the Relaxation Technique, you will also find that you are able to incorporate a visualization of yourself experiencing new attitudes and new successes. When you envision yourself positively, you will find yourself accomplishing your goals.

With all of these benefits, you might wonder why all the world is not engaged in this activity. Actually, many people are. Though learning to relax takes a bit of effort, time, and practice, it is really fun and well worth it. Think of relaxation as that part of your journey to overcoming math anxiety where you leisurely float down a slow-moving river, enjoying a feeling of timelessness. Are you ready to try reaching this relaxed state?

Ask someone to read the following Relaxation Technique to you or tape yourself reading it. Always speak softly and slowly, allowing plenty of time to pass at the pauses (indicated by ". . ."). Anything in parentheses should not be read aloud. Set up a comfortable situation for yourself by wearing loose clothing, unplugging the telephone, and putting up a "do not disturb" sign if you are likely to be interrupted. Either sit in a straight-backed chair with your feet flat on the ground and your hands on your lap, or sit yoga-style with your back against a wall, your legs crossed, and your hands on your lap. Your position should be comfortable enough to maintain for 15 or 20 minutes. Wear a sweater or use a blanket because your body tends to cool off as it slows down during relaxation.

RELAXATION TECHNIQUE

Begin by placing your feet flat on the floor.
Let your arms lie in a comfortable position on your lap.
Get very comfortable in your chair.
Now, close your eyes. . . .
Take three very deep breaths. . . . Inhale and feel your chest expand, then slowly exhale . . . inhale . . . exhale slowly . . . inhale . . . exhale slowly. . . . Good.
Continue to breathe deeply and fully.

Focus on your legs and tighten all the muscles in your toes . . . in your feet . . . your calves . . . your thighs . . . and your buttocks. Hold all of these muscles tight. Feel the tension in your leg muscles. Release and exhale. . . . Feel the relaxation as the tension leaves the muscles in your legs. . . . Remember this feeling of relaxation in your legs.

Tense your abdomen. Hold. . . . Feel the tension. . . . Release and exhale. . . . Feel the relaxation as the tension leaves your abdomen.

Now focus on your arms and tighten all the muscles in your fingers . . . in your hands . . . your arms . . . and your shoulders. Hold. . . . Feel the tension. . . . Release and exhale. . . . Feel the relaxation as the tension leaves the muscles in your arms. . . . Remember this feeling of relaxation in your arms.

Focus on your head. Tighten your neck muscles. Scrunch up your face by tightening your forehead . . . your eye muscles . . . your eyebrows . . . your cheeks . . . your nose . . . your lips . . . and clench your jaw. Hold. . . . Feel the tension. . . . Release and exhale. . . . Feel the relaxation as the tension leaves your face and neck.

Take a deep breath. As you breathe, feel the relaxation flow through your body like a wave. You become more relaxed as it passes through your head . . . back . . . down your neck . . . through your shoulders, arms, hands, and fingertips . . . and then down your back . . . your buttocks . . . through your thighs, calves, feet, and toes. Your body feels heavy. With each breath, it is getting heavier and heavier. You feel your body sinking, molding itself to the chair. You are getting more and more relaxed.

Your whole body feels full of relaxation. Take a deep breath. Enjoy this feeling of relaxation. Allow any thoughts that you have to simply pass through your mind. See these thoughts drifting away into space, as a balloon would drift away into the sky . . . getting smaller and smaller.

Imagine yourself stepping on an escalator and as it goes down, you become more and more relaxed. Imagine the escalator moving downward from the fifth floor. You can see the number four painted on the wall in front of you as you reach the fourth floor. Picture yourself going further down, approaching the third floor, becoming more relaxed. Visualize the number three painted on the wall. Continue going down becoming even more relaxed . . . two-ooo . . . deeper and deeper . . . and finally you arrive on the first floor, into a very peaceful and comforting place. It is a very special and private place of your own, which may exist in the real world or perhaps only in your imagination. It may be outdoors, by a stream and a meadow with the sounds of running water and the fragrance of wild flowers. Or perhaps it's a beach by the ocean with the sun warming you and hearing the sounds of the ocean waves, or perhaps it's in a cabin high up in the mountains with you curled up with a book in front of a warming fire. Imagine yourself in your special place. . . . Become aware of everything around you. What colors do you see? . . . What are the fragrances? . . . What do you hear? . . . Taste? . . . Enjoy the peace and the comfort of your special place. . . . Enjoy the relaxation that you are presently feeling . . . (wait about 15 seconds). . . . Allow yourself to enjoy your special place and the relaxation for a while . . . (wait anywhere between one and five minutes).

You are feeling very relaxed. Slowly imagine yourself leaving your special place, bringing the feeling of relaxation with you. In a few seconds, you will be asked to get back on the escalator. . . . Now, imagine yourself stepping on the escalator on the first floor, riding up slowly to the second floor. As you move up, you slowly become more and more aware of where you are . . . two-ooo . . . up to three-eee . . . four-rrr . . . beginning to feel the chair . . . fi-iiive. . . . Become more aware of your body. . . . Wiggle your toes and fingers, move your body, feel the chair you are sitting in. . . . You are becoming more alert. . . . Stretch and open your eyes. You are relaxed, yet full of energy!

What did you experience while doing the relaxation? How did you feel afterwards?

OTHERS:
I had a hard time visualizing a particular place.
I kept thinking that I really should be doing some work instead of sitting here.
I kept wondering if I was doing it right.
I kept thinking how stupid I must look.
I just felt a drifting sensation.
When Jim read it was time to come out of it, I didn't want to. I just wanted to stay in
     that relaxed state.
Afterwards, I felt calm and refreshed.
I'm disappointed that I couldn't get into it and become totally relaxed.

YOURS:
_____

_____

_____

_____

_____

_____

_____

_____

Were you able to experience a "floating" sensation? Even if you found yourself somewhat fidgety, you were probably able to relax enough to experience the benefits of this Relaxation Technique. It is a great luxury to take time out from the day for "me time": time to reflect, relax, and be still. It is a luxury that helps you get the most out of your busy schedule, when you return to it relaxed and focused.

It would be best to set time aside to practice your relaxation, hopefully each day, ideally twice a day. In planning your relaxation time, you might think about the fact that it should not be done right after a meal. Some people find that a morning relaxation is a wonderful way to start the day, while others find it the perfect way to relax before bed. Another option is to relax during the day, during a low-energy time, as a pick-me-up. If you are having difficulty finding the time for this important activity, don't feel frustrated, Chapter 8 will help you manage your time.

PRACTICE MAKES PERFECT!

When you practice the Relaxation Technique, you train your body to relax. The more you practice, the more easily and quickly you'll reach a relaxed state. The full Relaxation Technique has you tense all the muscles in your body so that through the muscle tension you can better experience the muscle relaxation. After you practice several times, you may find that you are able to relax your muscles without having to physically tense them first. You can alter the technique, leaving out those parts that ask you to tense, but including the sensation of having the tension leave the various parts of the body. Also, once you choose your special place, you don't have to include the suggestions of a meadow, beach, or cabin. You will be able to go to your special place directly. You will probably want to stay in your special place longer and longer each time you practice.

Since the relaxation experience gets better and better with practice, it is suggested that you schedule some time to relax each day. Some space is provided here for you to continue recording your experiences and reactions. (If more space is needed, it is provided in the journal in Appendix F.)

RELAXATION PRACTICE SESSIONS:

Date _____

Time _____

Your reactions: _____

_____

_____

_____

_____

Date _____

Time _____

Your reactions: _____

_____

_____

_____

_____

Date _____

Time _____

Your reactions:

_____

_____

_____

_____

_____

Once you become comfortable with the Relaxation Technique, you can begin to incorporate positive messages and visualization into the process. Being in a relaxed state makes you more willing to let in and believe positive statements. When you tell yourself positive statements about math while relaxing, you are more willing to accept them as true. It is exciting to find yourself suddenly believing, acting, and moving toward the math goals that you include in your relaxation!

Visualization, or picturing, is another way to begin to believe that you are good at math. *Seeing* oneself "acing" a math test with confidence will help it become a reality. Visualization may take a little practice, but it is well worth it.

Let's try to incorporate positive messages and visualization into a Relaxation Technique. To do this, you will have to repeat the full Relaxation Technique, only this time when you get to your special place, you should repeat a positive statement to yourself several times.

Choose one or more positive messages to use when you get to your special place in the Relaxation Technique.

OTHERS:

I feel comfortable while doing math.

Math comes easily to me.

I enthusiastically look forward to my math studies.

YOURS:

_____

_____

_____

_____

At the same time that you make this positive statement, you should try to visualize it becoming a reality. For example, if your positive message is "I feel comfortable while doing math," you can visualize yourself feeling confident while working math problems in a comfortable setting.

What picture are you going to create?

OTHERS:

I will see myself taking the test,
    feeling confident, and smiling.
I will see myself getting the test
    back with an "A" on it.

YOURS:

_____

_____

_____

_____

You should spend a few minutes in your special place, repeatedly giving yourself a positive message and visualizing it. Now try the full Relaxation Technique with your positive message and visualization.

What are your reactions to doing the Relaxation Technique with a positive message and visualization?

OTHERS:

I found myself feeling more sure about my positive statement.

My picture kept disappearing.

YOURS:

_____

_____

_____

_____

Keep up the good work and remember it all gets easier with practice.

RELAXING IN A JAM

There will be times, right before an exam, for example, when you find yourself tensing up and in need of relaxation. It would be impossible to take the time to do the full Relaxation Technique. We have just the solution. The following techniques list several steps that can be taken to achieve relaxation in a short period of time.

The Quickie Relaxation

1. Sit quietly and close your eyes.
2. Take three to five slow deep breaths. Inhale for four counts, hold for four counts, and exhale slowly for six or more counts.
3. Visualize your special place. This is a good time to give yourself positive messages as well.
4. When you feel ready, slowly open your eyes.

Of course there may also be times when you panic and there is no time to spare, such as in the midst of a math test. This is the time to get back into a relaxed state as quickly as possible.

The Quick Quickie Relaxation!

1. Close your eyes.
2. Take several slow and deep breaths.
3. Open your eyes.

Both quickie relaxations are most effective when you have been regularly practicing the full Relaxation Technique. Since, with practice, you will be used to settling down and relaxing, you can expect a quicker relaxation response from your body.

CONCLUSION

There are many different ways in which relaxation can help you overcome your math anxiety. First, relaxing helps reduce the physical experiences associated with math anxiety. You feel calmer, less tense, and your heartbeat slows. You can control your physical symptoms of anxiety. Second, you can give yourself positive messages while you are in a relaxed state. This makes them more real. You begin to believe them and make them true. Last, visualization, when combined with relaxation, helps you see yourself reaching your goals. As you hear your positive messages and envision yourself accomplishing these goals, you are likely to make them a reality.

You will probably agree that the Relaxation Technique is the most enjoyable of the five tools to overcoming math anxiety. You may also notice its spillover effects into your daily life. You will be physically and emotionally healthier, as well as have more energy to put into all of your work. Continue to relax daily, and you will see for yourself.

Chapter 6

Better Study Habits

On your journey to becoming free of math anxiety, the roads you have traveled in the preceding chapters have prepared you well for tackling a mathematics class. This chapter offers you further preparation in the form of study habits specifically geared for use in a math course.

"How will better study habits help reduce my math anxiety?" you may be saying to yourself. Improved study habits mean that you will be staying "on top of the math." You'll be organized, persistent in not only working a problem but also in seeking assistance. All of this will bring you a clearer understanding of math. And, if you can learn to actually understand the material, you will feel more confident and definitely less anxious. You will be better prepared for the test that usually gets your hands sweating. Math won't seem as confusing or mysterious to you. In fact, you will feel more in control. As if all of this isn't enough, you will in turn earn better grades and may be able to reach that career goal you aspire to.

This chapter on study techniques is divided into several subsections. It takes you from the classroom, on to homework and test preparation, and finally through the testing process.

IN THE CLASSROOM

The following exercise consists of study tips you can use in the classroom. After reading through them, take inventory of what you already do by checking the appropriate boxes. Pay special attention to those items that you have not checked off and plan to make improvements.

☐ **1. *Be sure that you are in the right class.***

Before delving into a math course, it is a good idea to make sure that the course begins at a level you are prepared to handle. Learning math is like building a house; you cannot build the house unless you have a good foundation. If you are lacking in math foundations, it will be difficult to learn new math skills because math builds on your knowledge of previous procedures.

For one reason or another you may have some mathematical gaps, such as fractions, decimals, or the multiplication tables. It is nothing to be ashamed of. Fortunately, you can fill these gaps by enrolling in a course that covers the skills you are lacking (perhaps an arithmetic course) or by working on your own (with a workbook). The benefits of taking a review class are that it offers structure, help from the teacher, contact with others who are similarly motivated, and use of any math laboratory facilities. Though for some this may mean going as far back as third grade math, you will find the effort well worth it. In fact, you will find that some of those concepts will be easier to grasp as an adult than they were when you were a child! Experience is on your side. Taking the time to go back to get a good math foundation will help you move more quickly through your program of study and toward your goal.

☐ **2. *Bring necessary tools to class.***

Bring paper, pencil and textbook to class. You will need paper and pencil in order to take notes. Your textbook is useful to have when your teacher refers to it in class, so you can easily follow the discussion. Bring a calculator if your class is using one. This study tip may seem simplistic, but it is essential!

☐ **3.** *Sit in the front two rows of the class.*

There are a lot of good reasons for sitting in the front of the class. First, you will be able to see and hear the teacher's presentation better. With good eye contact between you and the teacher, you may feel more comfortable relating to her both inside and outside of class. Second, you won't be easily distracted by the noise of others' conversations. It is a known fact that successful students are those who migrate to the front rows.

☐ **4.** *Have homework questions ready.*

You should never leave any questions unanswered! Have your questions from the homework and/or the reading clearly marked and ready to be asked. Often teachers set time aside in class to answer these questions. Use it! If you do not have time to get your questions answered in class, be sure to ask them after class. There are no stupid questions, and teachers appreciate your interest.

☐ **5.** *Take explanatory notes.*

Have you ever looked over your math class notes and realized that you did not understand what was going on in class? Often, students will write down only what appears on the blackboard. At the time it may seem sufficient, but not very long after the class is over, the notes may not be enough; you may not be able to bring it all back by looking at them. In fact, for a math class you need to include comments and explanations given by the teacher. If you do this, you will find your notes much easier to understand. Explanations will be clearly written and you will not have to depend totally on your memory. If you are an *active* notetaker, in the sense of recording most of the explanations, you will gain in several ways. First, you will be more alert in class; second, you will process more of what the teacher has said; and third, you will remember the steps better because you wrote them down.

Here is an example of what might be placed on the board in a classroom, and what should be recorded in a student's notes.

BOARD:

$$\frac{2}{15} + \frac{5}{6} = \qquad LCD = 30$$

$$\frac{2}{15} = \frac{2}{15} \cdot \frac{2}{2} = \frac{4}{30} \qquad \text{and} \qquad \frac{5}{6} = \frac{5}{6} \cdot \frac{5}{5} = \frac{25}{30}$$

$$SO, \qquad \frac{2}{15} + \frac{5}{6} = \frac{4}{30} + \frac{25}{30}$$

$$= \frac{29}{30}$$

NOTES:

Problem:
$$\frac{2}{15} + \frac{5}{6} =$$

Addition of fractions - needs LCD (Not needed for multiplication or division)

Step 1:
$$LCD = 30$$

What is the smallest number that both 15 and 6 divide into evenly?

Step 2:
$$\frac{2}{15} = \frac{2}{15} \cdot \frac{2}{2} = \frac{4}{30}$$

Rewrite fractions with LCD
Multiply numerator and denominator by 2

and,
$$\frac{5}{6} = \frac{5}{6} \cdot \frac{5}{5} = \frac{25}{30}$$

Multiply numerator and denominator by 5

Step 3:
$$so, \frac{2}{15} + \frac{5}{6} = \frac{4}{30} + \frac{25}{30}$$

Add numerator only (Keep same denominator)

$$= \frac{29}{30}$$

Always check to see if answer is reduced to lowest form.
This answer is.

Here are a few reminders about taking good lecture notes:

1. Be as neat as possible.
2. Write down your teacher's explanations as well as what is on the board.
3. Star or underline points that are stressed in class.
4. Fill in gaps as soon as possible after class.
5. Make sure that your notes could be read a week or two later and still be understood.

Taking good notes requires practice. During your next math lecture, see if you are able to follow the above suggestions. Then ask yourself the following questions about your notes:

Were you able to write fast enough to get what was written on the board as well as what the teacher was saying?

OTHERS:
I wrote as fast as I could, but I couldn't get all that the teacher said.

YOURS:
_____

_____

_____

_____

_____

Were you able to fill in any gaps in your notes right after class?

OTHERS:
I sat down right after class with a friend and filled in all of the empty spaces in my notes. I was really surprised when I remembered so much after class. I was glad I had left space
in my notes to do this.

YOURS:
_____

_____

_____

_____

_____

_____

Can you read and understand your lecture notes?

OTHERS:

My notes were pretty messy, so I rewrote them. They look pretty good now!

YOURS:

_____

_____

_____

_____

Could your notes be used for studying at a future date?

OTHERS:

Yes, I think that I could look at my notes two weeks from now and understand them. But before trying to take thorough notes, I would just look at my notes and see numbers, and not understand why any of them were there.

YOURS:

_____

_____

_____

_____

☐ **6. _Be attentive in class._**

Participate in class. Take the risk. If you know the answer to a question posed by the teacher, answer it. Also, if you are confused, let your teacher know by asking for an explanation, even if she has already given one. Asking questions and making mistakes are all part of learning math.

☐ **7. _Attend class regulary and be on time._**

Arrive at class a couple of minutes early in order to get organized. Open your notebook and write in the date. This way you will be ready to take notes when the lecture starts.

Avoid missing classes if possible. It's difficult to get the most out of class and to take good notes if you are not there. It's better not to have to depend on other people's notes. If you must miss a class, try to get the lecture taped or borrow a good notetaker's notes. Be sure to get the assignment from a classmate and do it before the next lecture.

Your teacher is likely to have his or her own policy about missing class lectures and tests. It is usually discussed in the first class meeting. Be sure you have this information written down in your notebook. If you miss several days of class, your teacher will probably want to talk to you. If you miss a test, you should notify the teacher immediately.

Which of the classroom study techniques did you check off because you are already doing them? List them below.

OTHERS:
I sit in the front of class.
I bring my pencil, paper and math book to class.
I go to class regularly.

YOURS:

_____

_____

_____

_____

_____

_____

_____

Which of the classroom study techniques that you did not check off are you willing to include in your study program?

OTHERS:

I don't usually have my homework questions ready. I will start bringing them to class.
I usually write down only what the teacher has on the board. I will also try to write down
what the teacher is saying as a form of explanation.

YOURS:

_____

_____

_____

_____

_____

_____

_____

HOMEWORK: WHERE, WHEN, AND HOW

Some of you may think that homework is some kind of punishment inflicted upon you by
your teacher. In actuality, when you do your homework, you become very active in the

learning process. You must first assimilate your lecture notes and the text reading so that you can work on the homework exercises. Then you must learn *how* to do the new type of problem. As you work, you get feedback on what you have successfully understood and what areas need more work. Continued practice enables you to become very familiar with new types of problems so that eventually you can work them automatically. The more you practice math, the better you will become. But, if you experience math anxiety, your first reaction to math homework may be to avoid doing it, or to put it off until the last minute. In this section, we focus on where, when, and how you should do your math homework so you will get the most out of your study time.

Where

Where you study math is important. It should be a comfortable place without a lot of other activity. First, let's examine where you are studying math right now.

List all of the physical locations where you study.

OTHERS:
bedroom
kitchen table
library
in front of TV

YOURS:
_____

_____

_____

_____

_____

Are the places you named both comfortable and quiet? If not, list two places where you could study that are good study environments (possibly one at school and one at home). Make a concerted effort to study math in these places.

OTHERS:
at my desk in my bedroom
library

YOURS:

_____

_____

_____

_____

_____

When

When you study math is also important. Because math requires both concentration and thought you'll want to study math at the time you ordinarily feel most alert. This is your peak time. People have a time of day during which they are energetic and best able to concentrate. You hear people state their peak times by saying, "I'm a morning person," or "I'm a late night person." Peak times can occur at any time of the day or night. It is best for you to study a difficult subject (math) during your peak time. Let's begin by examining the time of day you _now_ study math.

When are you presently studying math?

OTHERS:
late at night (10:00 p.m.)
after school (3:00 p.m.)

YOURS:

_____

_____

Now, think about when you are the most alert and energetic. What are your peak times of the day?

OTHERS:
morning, around 8:30 - 11:00 a.m.

YOURS:

_____

_____

_____

_____

It would be best to study math at your peak times. You will always find time to read an assignment from another course that you enjoy. If your present study time for math is not at a peak time, be sure to rearrange your schedule so that it is. You will have a clearer mind and the energy to tackle those math problems!

How

Here are some important suggestions on how to approach doing your homework. We must begin by saying, "Do it," since learning takes place through activity. You may already realize that doing your homework involves more than working the problems. Homework includes reading the textbook, reading your lecture notes, and working through the examples. Once you understand how the problems are worked, you must become familiar with them, learn to recognize them, and learn to distinguish them from other problems. Finally, you must practice them enough to be able to do them under pressure. The following 10 suggestions will help you maximize learning during your homework sessions. Check off those suggestions you already follow. Pay special attention to those items you have not checked off, and plan to make improvements by incorporating them into your homework sessions.

1. *Read your math book.*

If you are like most students, if the homework assignment is on page 23, you will open your math book to page 23 and begin working the problems. In doing so, you have passed up the valuable information on pages 1–22! In the actual text, you will find the author's explanation and some examples. Granted, reading your math text is not like reading your favorite novel. You must spend time with each paragraph, reading and rereading until you can follow what is being said. It is helpful to read with a pencil in hand so that you can write down your questions or write comments in the margins or so that you can summarize in your own words. You can underline helpful explanations and examples or important ideas. When you get to an example, you can fill in any steps that seem to be missing, and you can write the procedure in words beside the steps. Later, you can work some of the examples given in the text and then check your solution. This type of reading forces you to actively participate. It will make it easier for you to do the problems in the homework assignment when you get to page 23.

Since this is one study tip most students will find new and difficult, the following exercise is included to help you get started.

Before class

Before your next class, read the corresponding section of your math book. Don't worry if you don't understand it at this point. Remember that this is the first reading and you simply want to become acquainted with the material.

What section of your book will be covered in the next class?

OTHERS:
Chapter 4, section 4.2.

YOURS:

_____

What is the topic of this section?

OTHERS:

Least common multiples.

YOURS:

_____

What is the general idea of this reading? Write whatever you understand to be the main point or the basic procedure described. Again, don't worry if it's not perfectly clear at this point.

OTHERS:

The idea here is to find the smallest multiple that is common to two or more numbers. You have to list the multiples of each number until you find one that matches. This seems rather time consuming. How do you know how many multiples to list for each number?

YOURS:

_____

_____

_____

_____

_____

_____

Now that you have a general idea of what is going to be discussed in your next class, you have a foundtion to take good lecture notes.

After class

Did you feel that you had a better understanding of the lecture and took better notes having read the section ahead of time?

OTHERS:

It feels like I did understand the lecture a little bit better because I had thought about it and had formulated some questions. Also, the vocabulary was not so new to me, so I didn't have to think as much about the new words and could better concentrate on what the teacher was saying. Since it didn't seem so foreign to me, I was able to pay more attention in class than I had before.

YOURS:

_____

_____

_____

_____

_____

_____

_____

Now read the text again, marking it up as suggested in the discussion before the exercise. Look for the answers to questions you still have and write down any new questions that come to mind.

Here's a sample section from <u>Fundamentals of Math</u> by Arnold R. Steffensen and L. Murphy Johnson courtesy of HarperCollins Publishers, Inc.

4.2 LEAST COMMON MULTIPLES

1. Listing Method for finding the LCM

Recall from Section 2.1 that the multiples of a number are obtained by multiplying that number by each whole number. Consider the numbers 6 and 8. The nonzero multiples of 6 are

6, 12, 18, (24), 30, 36, 42, (48), 54, 60, 66, (72), ...   *— all common multiples*

and the nonzero multiples of 8 are

8, 16, (24), 32, 40, (48), 56, 64, (72), ...   *— def.*

* LCM of 6 and 8

Any number which is common to both lists on nonzero multiples is called a common multiple. The common multiples of 6 and 8 are

24, 48, 72, ...

The smallest of the common multiples of two (or more) counting numbers is called the **least common** *— def.*
multiple, or LCM, of the numbers. Since 24 is the smallest number in the list of common multiples of 6 and 8, we say that 24 is the LCM of 6 and 8. This method of finding the LCM of two or more numbers is called the **listing method.** When using the listing method, it is a good idea to use a chart to organize your work as shown below.

Multiples of 6	6	12	18	(24)	30	36	42
Multiples of 8	8	16	(24)				

* LCM is 24

Example 1   Finding the LCM Using the Listing Method

Find the LCM of the given numbers.

(a) 12 and 30

Multiples of 12	12	24	36	48	(60)	72	84
Multiples of 30	30	(60)					

* LCM is 60

We stop writing multiples of 30 once we find a multiple that is also in the first list. Since the smallest number common to both lists is 60, we say the LCM of 12 and 30 is 60.

(b) 6, 10 and 15

1) find several multiples of first two numbers
2) Be sure there is a common multiple of these before looking for a common multiple in all three

Multiples of 6	6	12	18	24	(30)	36	42
Multiples of 10	10	20	(30)	40	50	60	
Multiples of 15	15	(30)					

* LCM is 30

Since 30 is in the first two lists, we can stop after 30 in the third list. The LCM of 6, 10, and 15 is 30.

75

Were you able to find the answer to questions you still have?

OTHERS:

I understand perfectly how to find the LCM. I write the multiples of each number until I find one that matches. I don't see how this relates to the title of the chapter: Adding and Subtracting Fractions. I'll read the next section of the book and see if that helps.

YOURS:

_____

_____

_____

_____

_____

_____

_____

_____

Now that you have completed this exercise, you probably have begun to recognize the benefit of reading your math text. Did you notice how reading the text helps you to better understand the lecture, while the lecture helps you understand the text? Continue reading your math text in this way and you are sure to improve your understanding of the material you are studying.

☐ **2. *Read your lecture notes.***

Read your lecture notes as soon after class as possible, while it is still fresh in your mind. Fill in all those half-sentences you wrote when the teacher was talking faster than you could write. Fill in missing steps and explanations on how to get from one step to the next. Underline to emphasize important ideas and procedures.

Once you have completed your notes, they are an excellent resource. Use your lecture notes as you do your textbook—read and reread them and write down questions and comments. Good notes allow you to replay the class lecture as many times as you wish!

3. *Read directions carefully.*

The directions tell you what to do with a problem. If you skip or misread them, you may do the problem incorrectly, even though you know how to do it. Therefore, it is worth the time and effort it takes to read and understand the directions.

For instance, the directions may ask you to find the prime factorization for 24. If your answer is 4 x 6, you successfully found a factorization; but it is not the *prime* factorization. To find a *prime factorization*, you must continue factoring until all the factors are prime numbers. Since 4 = 2 x 2 and 6 = 2 x 3, we continue to factor 24 = 4 x 6 = (2 x 2) x (2 x 3) = 2 x 2 x 2 x 3 = 2^3 x 3. If you had not read the directions carefully, you might have stopped at 4 x 6, when the correct answer is 2^3 x 3.

In another problem, if you look at the algebraic expression $x^2 + 3x + 2$, without looking at the directions, you might automatically think to factor it into $(x + 1)(x + 2)$. This would be perfect if the directions say "factor." What if the directions say "evaluate the expression for $x = -1$"? Then $x^2 + 3x + 2 = (-1)^2 + 3(-1) + 2 = 1 - 3 + 2 = 0$. So the answer is 0, not $(x + 1)(x + 2)$.

Always read the directions before doing a problem. It is a good habit to develop. You can practice while doing your homework and it will help during a test.

4. *Name it.*

Identify the type of problem you are asked to solve. For example, you might name the problem 3.12 x 18.6 "decimal multiplication" or name the problem $(x^2 + 2x + 1)(x - 3)$ "product of polynomials." By naming each problem and saying the name to yourself before doing it, you are developing a habit that not only makes problem solving much easier, but makes test taking easier too. The payoff for this habit is sure to be great!

☐ **5. *Work carefully and neatly.***

Practice working carefully and neatly when you do your homework problems. Be on the lookout for those careless errors by checking each step before going on to the next step. This only takes a few seconds, but will help you catch your mistakes as they occur and prevent you from spending extra time on the problem working with the wrong numbers. You will be pleased to find yourself getting the right answer more often, and you won't become so frustrated. Your carefulness and neatness will be an asset during a test.

☐ **6. *Mark problem problems.***

After you have given it your best try, and then one more, mark any problems that you are still unable to do. *Do not* erase your wrong attempts. You can help your teacher pinpoint where your trouble lies by showing him or her your work and where you got stuck. If you are aware of your specific difficulties, you will feel less overwhelmed by a general sense that "I can't do it." You can tackle those specific difficulties and will find that you can indeed work those problems you thought were too difficult.

☐ **7. *Get all questions answered.***

Remember that you have questions marked in your book, in your notes, and in your homework. These should all be answered, no matter how small they seem or how many there are. Ask during class or after class, as soon as you can. Do not let them build up until the day before the final exam!

☐ **8. *Work with others.***

This is a good method for studying. Others can help you with your difficult areas and you can help them with theirs. You will be amazed at how much you learn when explaining something to a friend. If everyone is having trouble, it will be a good experience to figure it out together. Keep in mind that to get the most out of study groups, everyone should come prepared, having read the material, tried the problems, and studied on their own.

☐ **9. *Review frequently.***

If you want to make test preparation easier, take time at the end of each week to work some problems from the previous sections. This will force you to look at problems over and over, until you are eventually able to recognize and work them immediately. You will also begin to compare last week's problems with this week's problems, recognizing differences and similarities between them. You will develop a familiarity and facility with the material that will make preparation for a test, and the test itself, much easier.

☐ **10. *Get missed assignments.***

Be sure to get the assignment from any class you miss. You should have at least one classmate whom you can depend on to give you the notes or a tape of the lecture, and any assignments given. Be sure to review these notes and do the assignment before the next class, so that you won't fall behind.

Which homework study techniques did you check off because you are already doing them? List them below.

OTHERS:

I read all of the directions carefully when I'm doing my homework.

I often do my homework with friends. (Sometimes we goof off though, when the assignment is difficult).

I mark problem problems. I always mark the problems that I don't know, but I don't always get the help I need to answer them.

YOURS:

_____

_____

_____

_____

_____

_____

_____

Which homework study techniques that you did not check off are you willing to include in your study program?

OTHERS:

I am actually ready to start reading my textbook.

I like the idea of "naming the problem" and think that it would be a great help to me.

I commit to getting my homework questions answered. I mark them with the intention of getting them answered but find it too time consuming to actually do that. I will put forth the time and effort to get them answered.

YOURS:

_____

_____

_____

_____

_____

_____

_____

_____

STUDYING FOR AN EXAM

There is a great deal of anxiety associated with taking a math test. Usually, if you are extraordinarily anxious over this particular event, it is because you are caught up in an anxiety cycle.

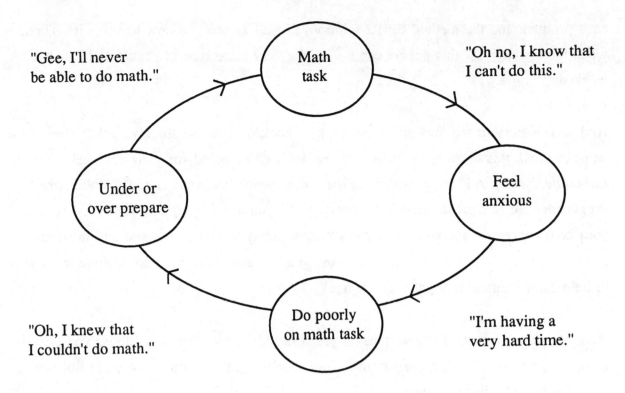

Figure 2. The test anxiety cycle.

Right when the teacher hands you your math test, you may begin thinking, "I"ve got to do well today. My last test was so hard. Maybe I should've studied more. Oh no, I don't recognize this problem!" You are feeling anxious, panic-stricken, and may be "blanking out"! You hear yourself saying, "What am I going to do?" You start jumping from problem to problem, unable to concentrate well enough to complete much of anything. Of course, when your test is returned, you have a poor grade. Anxiety clearly prevented you from thinking clearly and performing well. What happens next? As you prepare for the next test, your thoughts of the last test may make you either underprepare or overprepare. You may avoid studying because you just don't want to face the math (then you can tell yourself that failure is due to lack of studying, not lack of knowledge), or delay studying so you are not very well prepared. When you do study, worries about the test may make it difficult to concentrate, so your study sessions are not very productive.

Another possibility is that your anxiety makes you overprepare. This is a term used for someone who spends many hours working problem after problem after problem, but who does so frantically. This person skips the real review process in which you think about each problem and the method for its solution, as well as practice how to solve it. Then, when the test arrives, this person can't work the very same type of problems he or she worked at home.

And so it is easy to see how someone can get "hooked" into the anxiety cycle. One of the ways to break this cycle is to make sure you are well prepared for your next test. You should be careful to keep up with your daily homework assignments and to follow the suggestions for test preparation in this section. If you are thorough in your preparation, your confidence will increase, and you are more likely to remain relaxed and in control during the test. If you start to feel anxious, you can use relaxation and positive messages to help calm yourself and get back on track.

Here are some important suggestions on preparing for a test. Check off those you already include as part of your test preparation. Pay special attention to those you are not doing, and plan to make improvements.

☐ **1. *Make a study schedule.***

Begin to study approximately one week prior to a test. You should make a schedule, listing those sections in the book that you will study each day. Schedule a sample test to be taken upon completion of those sections. This sample test should be taken two days before the test date so that you have time to work on any areas of difficulty. Except for a general review, there should be nothing left to study the day before the exam.

☐ **2. *Rework problems.***

You should actively prepare for a test. Do more than read your notes and the textbook. Do more than look over your homework. Actually *rework* problems from each section of your book. Be especially conscious of the directions and take note of the type of problem that you are working.

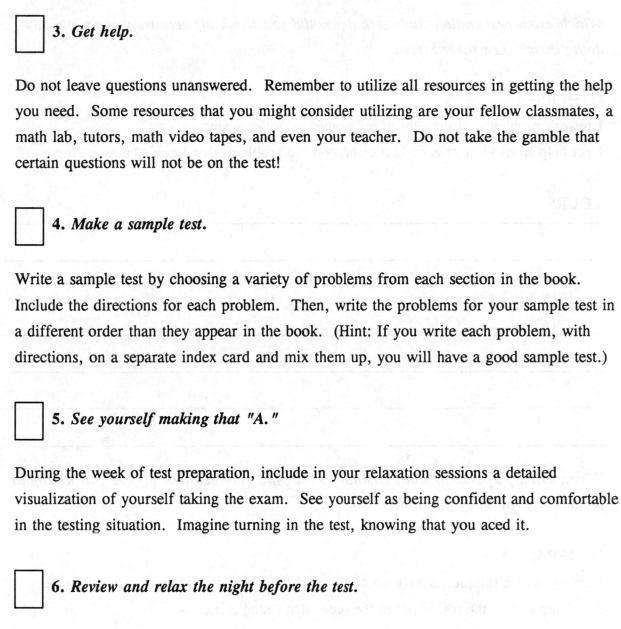

3. *Get help.*

Do not leave questions unanswered. Remember to utilize all resources in getting the help you need. Some resources that you might consider utilizing are your fellow classmates, a math lab, tutors, math video tapes, and even your teacher. Do not take the gamble that certain questions will not be on the test!

4. *Make a sample test.*

Write a sample test by choosing a variety of problems from each section in the book. Include the directions for each problem. Then, write the problems for your sample test in a different order than they appear in the book. (Hint: If you write each problem, with directions, on a separate index card and mix them up, you will have a good sample test.)

5. *See yourself making that "A."*

During the week of test preparation, include in your relaxation sessions a detailed visualization of yourself taking the exam. See yourself as being confident and comfortable in the testing situation. Imagine turning in the test, knowing that you aced it.

6. *Review and relax the night before the test.*

The night before the exam is best used *reviewing* the material. This may include working one problem from each section or simply reworking problems that have given you difficulty. It may also help you to think through procedures needed to solve problems, without actually writing anything down. After this review, spend time relaxing, whether it be watching TV, taking a hot bath, or doing the Relaxation Technique. Also be sure to eat well and get a good night's sleep.

Which exam preparation study techniques did you check off because you are already doing them? List them below.

OTHERS:

I rework problems. I do a lot of my homework over again.

I get help from some friends in the class on the problems that I don't know.

YOURS:

_____

_____

_____

_____

_____

_____

_____

Which exam preparation study techniques that you did not check off are you willing to include in your study program?

OTHERS:

I never make a sample test. It would be good for me to do this because I always get
> upset that the test is not in the order that I studied it.

I don't ever imagine myself getting that "A." I always see myself failing the test, and
> then I actually do fail the test. I will definitely try to see myself being successful.

I always stay up late the night before the exam working more problems. I'm going to try
> to relax and get a good night's sleep.

YOURS:

_____

_____

_____

_____

_____

_____

_____

_____

_____

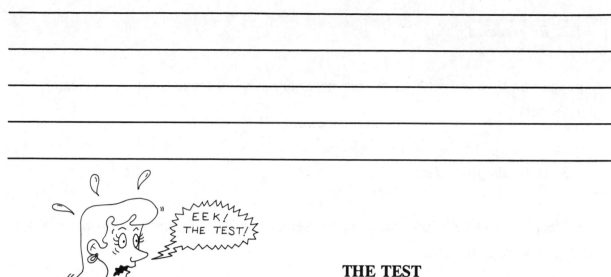

THE TEST

Test time can be very anxiety producing, but it does not have to be. A lot of people tend to place too much importance on a test, feeling that one test alone will make or break their entire grade for the class, their college major, or even their life career choice. By placing that much emphasis on a test, one will aggravate the anxiety, which makes it more difficult to concentrate and perform well. You then find yourself hooked into the anxiety cycle once again. If you have come prepared, you can focus on the positive and remind yourself that you are ready to take this test. A really good attitude to have is one in which you see the test as both a challenge and an opportunity to show what you have learned.

Check off those suggestions that you are presently doing. Pay special attention to those you are not and make improvements.

☐ **1. *Arrive early.***

Arrive early enough to do a quickie relaxation before the test begins. If you feel uncomfortable relaxing in your classroom, try the restroom or go outside and sit under a tree. You can first visualize your special place and then visualize yourself sitting through the test, feeling very confident and comfortable, and knowing that you made an "A." Positive statements to yourself will help, too.

☐ **2. Be prepared.**

Be in class on time and with all of your necessary supplies (pencil, paper, calculator, ruler, eraser).

☐ **3. Write the formulas.**

If you feel it would be helpful, write down memorized formulas on your test paper before you begin working the test.

☐ **4. Read the directions.**

Make sure you understand what is being asked of you; if not, be sure to ask for clarification.

☐ **5. Do what you know best, first.**

Look over the test and begin by working problems that you consider easy. This will help you keep your confidence. Plus, if time runs out, you answered as many questions correctly as you possibly could. This way there aren't any questions that you would have gotten correct but didn't have the time to do.

☐ **6. Name it.**

For each question, *name the type of problem* and ask yourself "What method do I need to solve this problem?" and "What should the end result look like?" (For example, this is a linear equation. I need to solve for x by getting it by itself on one side of the equation. My answer should be a number.)

☐ **7. Be neat.**

You will often earn more points if you teacher can easily read your test. Include all your steps in a neat and orderly fashion. Clearly mark your answer by placing it in the answer blank or by circling it.

☐ **8. Watch for careless errors!**

Under the pressure of a test, it is all too easy to make those dumb mistakes like copying the wrong number, adding $2 + 3$ and getting 6, or dropping a minus sign! Remember to check for accuracy as you work through each step (as you have practiced while doing your homework).

☐ **9. Move on.**

Move on if you get stuck. You may find that taking a break from the problem helps you solve it when you work on it a second time.

☐ **10. Try everything.**

Do not erase the work you have done just because you have not answered the problem completely. Sometimes, even writing the formula will earn you partial credit.

☐ **11. Remember to relax.**

If you find yourself developing symptoms of anxiety, put your pencil down and do your quick quickie relaxation.

☐ **12.** *Give yourself positive messages.*

Give yourself positive messages while taking the test. If you have forgotten, here is a list of some suggestions for you to tell yourself.

a. "My, I'm nervous; I can't even add 2 + 3. I'll stop for a second and do a quick quickie relaxation. Breathe in slowly, then release. Now that's better."

b. "This is just like a problem I did yesterday. Since I've done one like it, I know I can do this one, too."

c. "Is this a trick question? No, it must use a technique or method that we studied. If it doesn't come to me, I'll skip it now and perhaps I can get it later."

☐ **13.** *Hold on to that test.*

Do not be fooled by the person who turns his or her paper in very early; it is usually a student who does not know the material and has skipped most of the problems. Most often it is the "A" student (you, for example) who keeps his or her paper to the end.

Use the extra time to check your work. Ask yourself these questions: Did I answer the question asked? (For example, if the problem asks for the number of boys, do not write down the number of girls.) Does my answer make sense? (For example, you cannot have -3 boys!) Can I verify my answer? (For example, if you had to solve the equation $2x + 1 = 7$ and found $x = 4$, when you plug 4 back into the equation in place of x, you will find $2(4) + 1 = 9$ -- you made a mistake.) Look over your steps to make sure they make sense and can be read easily.

☐ **14.** *Be responsible.*

If you know in advance that something is going to prevent you from taking the exam, discuss the matter with your teacher ahead of time.

Which test taking techniques did you check off because you are already doing them?
List them below.

OTHERS:

I arrive early.

I always write all of the formulas down first. I'm always worried that I might forget them, so I write them down before I start the test.

I usually move on to the next problem if I get stuck for awhile.

YOURS:

_____

_____

_____

_____

_____

_____

_____

_____

Which test taking techniques that you did not check off are you willing to include in your study program?

OTHERS:

I will read the directions. Usually, I'm in such a hurry because I'm worried about the time, that I don't bother to read the directions.

I will work all of the problems that I know best, first. I sometimes realize that I don't even see many of the problems that I know.

I will hold on to the test until the end of the class period. Many times I am so glad to be finished with the test that I don't want to look at it another second and so I turn it in without proofing it.

YOURS:

_____

_____

_____

_____

_____

_____

_____

POST TEST

Since testing is a part of the learning process, what you do with your returned test is very important. Check off those suggestions below that you are presently doing and make improvements in those that you are not.

☐ **1. _Correct the returned test._**

Correct your test while it is still fresh in your mind. Do not erase your work on the test. Do not write corrections on the test itself, but write corrected answers on a separate sheet of paper and staple the corrections to your test. Check to be sure you have reworked the problems correctly.

☐ **2. _See your teacher._**

See your teacher if the grading is unclear to you or if, after trying to correct it, you still do not understand a problem.

☐ **3.** *Analyze mistakes.*

Analyze your mistakes to see if there are any common patterns. Your teacher can help you recognize these patterns.

☐ **4.** *Use the test for review.*

Use your test to test yourself again in preparation for the final exam.

Which post test study techniques did you check off because you are already doing them? List them below.

OTHERS:

I use the test for a review for the final.

I must admit that I used to just look for my grade but lately I've been correcting the
      problems that I missed.

YOURS:

_____

_____

_____

_____

_____

_____

_____

_____

Which post test techniques that you did not check off are you willing to include in your study program?

OTHERS:

I will correct the problems that I missed.

I will analyze my mistakes to see if there is any pattern in my errors.

YOURS:

_____

_____

_____

_____

_____

_____

_____

_____

CONCLUSION

You might be saying to yourself, "How can I include all of these 'shoulds' in my life? There are only 24 hours in a day!" It is true that the list of recommendations in this chapter is a long and healthy one, but we expect that you already practice many of them. You have already incorporated these into your study program. You can do the same for the new "shoulds" that you choose to use. Make it a priority to do them, and soon they will become a part of your life.

Good luck and happy studying!

Chapter 7

Better Problem-Solving Skills

Have you ever sat staring at a problem without any idea as to how to solve it? Of course you have. Everybody has this experience, including math majors and even math professors. But not knowing how to proceed does not mean you won't eventually figure it out. Rather than readily skipping over the problem and saying, "I haven't a clue," you can train yourself to stick with it, keep thinking, and continue trying. The tips and discussion in this chapter are intended to help you better understand and better attack problem-solving. The better your problem-solving skills, the more success you will have in math and the less anxiety you will experience.

When certain kinds of problems are presented in a math class, the teacher demonstrates one or more techniques for finding the solution. Sometimes a student thinks that if he can understand the technique as the teacher writes it on the board, he will have no trouble when doing it on his own. While it is certainly possible to understand new material right away, it is more likely that you will need to do much work before gaining a true understanding of how to work the problem. Even though everything looks very clear while in class, you may find "holes" in your understanding as you try to work the same type of problem on your own. This is normal. Doesn't a professional athlete make his or her sport look very easy? What happens when a novice tries a sport? Would you expect that he or she could do it as well, as gracefully, as skillfully, or as quickly as the pro? Of course not! As a math student, you are a math novice and your teacher is the pro. You need the same long hours, hard work, and practice that an athlete needs to perfect a sport.

NAMING A PROBLEM

There are so many types of math problems, with accompanying rules and formulas, that the whole subject can be overwhelming. If you classify each problem by giving it a name, a set of ten problems of the same nature essentially becomes one problem.

Thus, as you learn to solve a new type of problem, it is very helpful to "name it" and to use that name everytime you do such a problem. For example, the following arithmetic problem can be named "adding fractions."

$$\frac{1}{2} + \frac{1}{3}$$

Now this may seem obvious and simplistic, but naming and verbalizing helps you distinguish this problem from a similar looking problem.

$$\frac{1}{2} \cdot \frac{1}{3}$$

Here you are "multiplying fractions." In both problems, you are combining two fractions, but the process for combining the fractions is completely different for each.

ADDING FRACTIONS   MULTIPLYING FRACTIONS

$$\frac{1}{2} + \frac{1}{3}$$ $$\frac{1}{2} \cdot \frac{1}{3}$$

Have you ever made a mistake like this? $\frac{1}{2} + \frac{1}{3} = \frac{1}{6}$

Naming the problem "adding fractions" reminds you to follow the rules for *addition*, not multiplication, of fractions. If you have a name for each type of problem, all the rules and procedures will be more organized under headings in your mind. When you have a problem to solve, but have not given it a name, you must sort through all of these methods randomly. If you do give the problem a name, then the appropriate method will easily follow.

For example, in the problem, the name "adding fractions" reminds you to follow a procedure in which you first find a least common denominator.

$$\frac{1}{2} + \frac{1}{3} = \frac{2}{6} + \frac{3}{6} = \frac{5}{6}$$

Similarly, the name "multiplying fractions" reminds you that the correct procedure is to multiply numerators and denominators. (Do not find the least common denominator.)

$$\frac{1}{2} \cdot \frac{1}{3} = \frac{1 \cdot 1}{2 \cdot 3} = \frac{1}{6}$$

WRITING THE PROCEDURE

In naming a problem you have begun to put math into *words*! Suddenly a problem with numbers and other symbols becomes an idea with an associated task. Since many of you feel more comfortable with words than numbers, the more you do this, the better you can relate to math!

Think about the method used to solve a problem. What steps are involved every time you solve this type of problem? Write the procedure for solving a particular type of problem using your own words. Make sure the method makes sense to you personally.

Let's practice writing the procedure for a problem.

Problem:

$$\frac{1}{2} + \frac{1}{3}$$

Name: adding fractions

Method: Step 1. Find the least common denominator (LCD), if the denominators are not the same.

Step 2. Rewrite each fraction using the LCD.

Step 3. Add numerators (but not denominators).

Step 4. Reduce resulting fraction, if possible.

If necessary, you can go into more detail in any of the steps that you feel need more explanation. For instance, you may want to write down how to find the LCD that was mentioned in Step 1. Either subdivide Step 1 or write a whole new procedure with its own name, "Finding the LCD."

USING THE NAMING PROCESS WITH WRITING THE PROCEDURE

We recommend that you name new problems and write out the procedure for solving them. Then be sure to use the name and think about the procedure each time you work a problem. Say each step of the procedure to yourself as you do it. The time spent and the effort made will be well worth it. You should find yourself better understanding the method of solution and in time you should find yourself solving math problems with much greater ease and increased accuracy.

When you encounter a new type of problem, you can create an index card with the NAME at the top, the METHOD in words, and an example on the back (and perhaps reference the page number from your textbook). As you use your index cards in working problems, you will become more familiar with them and may begin to visualize them in your mind. Eventually you will not need to refer to the index cards themselves because the information will be in your head. If you can organize it this way, you will find problem-solving much easier.

As you practice, you should notice how this process helps you both to differentiate one type of problem from another and to focus on the proper method for finding the solution. We saw this in the two problems in which we added or multiplied two fractions. To further illustrate this point, we will work several more examples that closely resemble one another. The arithmetic examples are followed by examples from algebra. Read through those that are appropriate to your level and then do the exercises that follow the examples.

Let's compare two problems concerning the combining of integers.

1. Add (-2) + (-5)
2. Multiply (-2)(-5)

The integers are the same, but the operations are different. Now let's name them.

<table>
<tr><td>ADDING INTEGERS</td><td>MULTIPLYING INTEGERS</td></tr>
<tr><td>(-2) + (-5)</td><td>(-2)(-5)</td></tr>
</table>

Though it is clear that one problem asks that we add and the other asks that we multiply, we could easily make a mistake if we neglect to concentrate on the type of problem and its associated method for solution. Let's practice writing the method and solving the problems.

Problem:	Add (-2) + (-5)
Name:	addition of integers
Method:	Case 1. If the integers have the same sign, then add the unsigned numbers together and keep the sign.
	Case 2. If the integers have different signs, then subtract the unsigned numbers and keep the sign of the larger (unsigned) number.
Work the problem:	(-2) + (-5) = -7

Since -2 and -5 have the same sign, we followed Case 1. The answer is -7.

Problem:	Multiply (-2)(-5)
Name:	multiplication of integers
Method:	Case 1. If the integers have the same sign, then multiply the unsigned numbers; the answer is positive.
	Case 2. If the integers have different signs, then multiply the unsigned numbers; the answer is negative.
Work the problem:	(-2)(-5) = 10

Since -2 and -5 have the same sign, we followed Case 1. The answer is 10.

If we were working too fast, without thinking or saying the rules to ourselves, it would be easy to get the wrong answer by mixing up the rules for addition and multiplication.

Now let's compare two algebra problems.

1. Solve for x: $2x + 4x - 3 = 3$
2. Solve for x: $2x^2 + 4x - 3 = 3$

Do you see the similarities and the differences in these problems and their directions? Now let's name each of them.

<u>SOLVING A LINEAR EQUATION</u>   <u>SOLVING A QUADRATIC EQUATION</u>
$2x + 4x - 3 = 3$ $2x^2 + 4x - 3 = 3$

Naming the problem forces you to take a moment to prepare a game plan. Let's work each of these problems, after writing its method of solution.

Because the first problem has an equal sign, it is an *equation*. Since the highest power of the variable x is one, it is a *linear equation*. In order to solve a linear equation, you must look for a number that will replace x and make the equation true. The answer will be "$x = $ something".

Problem: Solve for x. $2x + 4x - 3 = 3$

Name: solving a linear equation

Method: Step 1.   Combine like terms on each side of the equation.

               Step 2.   Add (or subtract) the same terms to both sides of the equation as necessary, to separate variable terms from constant terms.

               Step 3.   Multiply (or divide) the same factor on both sides of the equation, in order to isolate the variable completely.

Work the problem: $2x + 4x - 3 = 3$

$$6x - 3 = 3$$
$$6x = 6$$
$$x = 1$$

The answer is $x = 1$.

The second problem is also an *equation*, but this time we have a *quadratic equation*, instead of a *linear equation*. It is quadratic because x is raised to the second power. Here you look for (up to two) numbers to replace x and make the equation true. This answer should also say "$x = $ something," but the method is different for solving this type of equation!

Problem: Solve for x. $2x^2 + 4x - 3 = 3$

Name: solving a quadratic equation

Method: Step 1. Put the equation in the form $ax^2 + bx + c = 0$, if it is not already.

Step 2. Factor the left side of the equation, if possible.

Step 3. If you can factor,

a. set each factor equal to zero.

b. solve each of the resulting linear equations for x.

Step 4. If you cannot factor, use the quadratic formula to solve for x.

Work the problem: $2x^2 + 4x - 3 = 3$

$2x^2 + 4x - 6 = 0$

$2(x^2 + 2x - 3) = 0$

$2(x - 1)(x + 3) = 0$

$2(x - 1) = 0$ or $(x + 3) = 0$

$x = 1$ or $x = -3$

The answers are $x = 1$ or $x = -3$.

The process is completely different for solving these two types of equations. Their only difference in appearance is an exponent of 2, yet the process for solving them and their answers are completely different.

Once you begin naming problems and writing down the method for solution, you may notice that you understand the procedures better. The process of writing the method involves thinking about each step. You will begin to ask why one step follows another and think about the results to expect. If you have questions, you can be more specific in asking them of yourself or a teacher. Rather than saying, "I don't understand this problem at all," you can ask "*Why* do you set each factor equal to zero in Step 3a?" Since knowing *what* to ask is half the battle, you will be in a better position to understand the answer to your question. You will be on your way to understanding the problems that you are studying.

Now it is time for you to practice naming and writing the procedure. Pick two problems (use problems that you are currently studying in class). Write the problem, its name, and the method for finding its solution. Then work the problem, following the steps you outlined in the method.

Problem 1:
_____

_____

_____

Name:
_____

Method:
_____

_____

_____

_____

_____

_____

_____

Work the problem:

_____

_____

_____

_____

_____

_____

_____

_____

_____

Problem 2:

_____

_____

_____

Name:

_____

Method:

_____

_____

_____

_____

_____

_____

_____

_____

Work the problem:

_____

_____

_____

_____

_____

_____

_____

_____

Now that you have practiced naming and writing the procedure at least twice, are you beginning to see the benefits? Did it force you to make sure that you understood a problem before trying to solve it? Did it help you to work slow enough to reduce the number of careless errors? How did you feel about talking to yourself as you said each of the steps?

OTHERS:

Well, I only worked two problems and I'm already tired of all the writing. It seems like a lot of extra work. But I did begin to understand what I was doing, so I think in the end it will be worth it. I forgot to say each step as I did it, but I will try to do it in the future. I will try anything that might help me make fewer careless mistakes!

YOURS:

_____

_____

_____

_____

_____

_____

_____

MEMORIZING FORMULAS

In mathematics, there are always rules and formulas to remember. The easier it is for you to memorize formulas, the more comfortable you will be with math. In general, the more you can understand about a method, rule, or formula, the better you will remember it. So, if possible, try to understand the derivation of a formula. (This is not always easy to do!) For example, the geometric formula for the perimeter of a rectangle refers to the distance around it, like the fencing around a yard. It is twice the length plus twice the width: $P = 2L + 2W$. If you look at a diagram of a rectangle, and think about the perimeter, you will easily note that the perimeter is found by taking Width + Width + Length + Length. This is more succinctly written as $2L + 2W$. If you ever forget the formula, your understanding of its meaning and derivation will help you remember it.

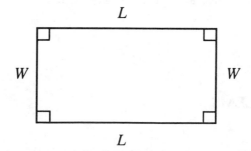

Memory techniques can be very helpful in memorizing formulas: Do you notice any patterns? Can you make up a little jingle? Can you relate it to something you already know? Many students use the phrase "Please Excuse My Dear Aunt Sally" to remember the Order of Operations rule for simplifying an expression. The first letter of each of the words in the phrase stands for the steps in the mathematical formula. Therefore, the order of operations is: first do all the operations in Parentheses; then simplify any Exponential expressions; then do any Multiplications or Divisions as they occur, working from left to right; then do any Additions or Subtractions as they occur, working from left to right. For example, $3 - 2 \times 4 + 10 \div 2 = 3 - 8 + 5 = 0$. Through another memory technique, most algebra students learn to multiply two binomials using the FOIL method: multiply First terms, Outside terms, Inside terms, and Last terms and then add resulting terms together. For example, $(x + 2)(x - 5) = x^2 - 5x + 2x - 10 = x^2 - 3x - 10$.

Finally, you will be surprised at how easy it can be to remember something you repeatedly use. If you want to learn a new formula, begin by saying the formula to yourself each time you work a problem. If you continue working several problems in this way, you should find yourself referring to the formula less and less, until eventually you know it by heart. Even a complicated formula like the quadratic formula (see below) can be memorized in this way; saying "find x by taking the opposite of b, plus or minus the square root of b squared minus $4ac$, all divided by $2a$" each time you use it.

$$x = \frac{-b \pm \sqrt{b^2 - 4ac}}{2a}$$

The next time you have to memorize a formula, try to understand its derivation, use memory techniques where possible, and practice saying it to yourself as you use it in several problems.

SOLVING WORD PROBLEMS

Many times you will encounter a problem that requires a little extra work, beyond simply naming it and following a specific procedure. Word problems fit into this category. Such problems force us to think harder and more creatively in order to find the pieces of the puzzle that fit together to form a solution. These are the types of problems that many students find frustrating, if not impossible. But there is hope if you are willing to try and allow yourself to fail, to practice and practice some more. When you attempt word problems, you gain familiarity with them and with the type of thinking involved.

In real life, many problems are expressed in words but require math for their solution. The word problems you encounter in math class illustrate how math can be used to solve a variety of problems, using techniques that you have already learned. The key is to translate the words in a problem into mathematical language.

You won't need much guidance for solving a problem that you already know how to solve. Though there is no one way to approach solving word problems, you may find the following of help when you find yourself stuck. The trick is to stay calm, to avoid being intimidated by the length or complication of a word problem. Though it may require a great deal of thought, remind yourself that it doesn't need to be done in your head, all in one instant, or even correctly the first try. You must allow yourself the freedom to take your time. You may need to play with the ideas, perhaps using trial and error, guessing, diagrams, or whatever helps you to further understand the problem.

The difficult part of solving a word problem is not so much in finding the final answer but in discovering the strategy you will use to find that answer. If it is an arithmetic problem, you will look for the correct operations and in algebra you will set up an appropriate equation(s). What follows is a six-step guide for solving arithmetic and algebraic word problems. It is braided with an example, showing how each of the steps can be applied.

Steps to Solving a Word Problem

Example:
Suppose five people go out to dinner and run up a bill of $125. If they want to include a 15% tip for the waiter and split the bill evenly, how much should each person contribute?

Step 1. Identify the type of problem.

Read the problem a couple of times. In this initial reading of the problem, see if you can give it a name. Arithmetic applications may be dealing with sales, real estate, taxes, gas mileage, conversion to or from metric, and so on. Algebraic applications tend to deal with distance, geometry, mixtures, and so on. Once you classify a problem, you will begin to think about formulas that may be relevant, similar problems that you have seen, and strategies that have worked for you in the past.

Example: This problem deals with figuring out a restaurant bill.

Step 2. Get a grasp of the problem.

Read the problem again several times and try to get a general idea as to what is going on. You will find it helpful to do the following.

    a. Look up or figure out unfamiliar words or concepts.

    b. Write down the question in words.

    c. Write down all the given information.

    d. Draw a diagram or sketch, if possible.

        Try to picture the situation in your head. Draw a diagram or sketch and label it with given information. It might be useful to put the information in a chart.

    e. If you are using algebra, identify the variable(s) in words.

        If a problem cannot be solved by using arithmetic operations alone, you can use algebra. A variable represents an unknown quantity in a problem. If you introduce a variable, say x, then you should explicitly state what it represents. This is a very important step that many would rather skip because it seems too easy. Writing something like "x = Bob's age" helps you focus on using the variable correctly when you set up an equation in the next step. Later, once you have solved for x, you will know exactly what you have found and you can use it to answer the question that you wrote in Step 2b!

Example:

    a. If you were not familiar with the concept of a tip, you would have to learn this before being able to solve the problem.

b. Find how much money each person must pay.

c. The bill is for $125. The tip will be 15% of the bill.

d. Draw a diagram.

e. We can figure this out with arithmetic and won't need to use algebra.

Step 3. Determine a strategy/Write the equation(s).

No one can tell you exactly how to come up with a plan for finding the solution, but if you are willing to play with the problem and make mistakes, you should eventually figure it out. Finding a plan is the hardest step in solving a word problem, but you have already begun to work on it while grasping the problem. You must pull out an appropriate formula, decide on which information to use and where to use it, and recognize inherent relationships or hidden information. Don't be shy about doing whatever is necessary to increase your understanding of a problem or about trying different possibilities. This is all a part of the problem-solving process. You may need to reread, redraw, and keep thinking, until you figure out what formula, operation or series of operations, or in algebra, what equation(s) will lead you to the answer.

Sometimes it is helpful to think about the problem with different numbers. If the numbers are made smaller or easier to work with, it is often easier to know how to go about answering the question. You can then apply the same strategy to the original problem, with the original numbers.

At other times, it is helpful to make several guesses at an answer, refining your guess each time until you eventually find the answer by trial and error. If you are also interested in a strategy that will apply to similar problems, the process of trial and error can sometimes help you to better understand the problem and figure out a strategy for solution.

If you need to take a break from the problem after having thought about it for some time, go ahead. Sometimes you come up with a strategy for solution during this time away. It's fantastic when you say "Ah ha!" and then go back to the problem to complete it.

Example:
We can do this in two ways. Strategy (a) is to first find the tip, 15% of $125. We'll add the amount of the tip to the bill to get a total amount. Finally, we'll divide the total amount by 5 to get the answer. Strategy (b) is to first divide the $125 by 5 to get the amount each person owes for the dinner, without the tip. Then we'll find the tip for each person by taking 15% of that amount. Finally, we'll add the two numbers together to get the amount each person owes.

Step 4. Use the strategy to work the problem/Solve the equation(s).

In an arithmetic problem, you would now work the problem by performing the operations. In algebra, solve the equation(s) using the appropriate procedure (for a linear equation, quadratic equation, system of equations, and so on).

Example:

Strategy (a):   The tip is 15% of $125. Thus, you should multiply $125 x 0.15 = $18.75. (Note that in a restaurant, you may need to do this in your head. You can take 10% of $125, which is $12.50; and then take 5% of $125, which is half the $12.50 which equals $6.25. Adding $12.50 + $6.25 = $18.75.) So the waiter should receive $18.75. The total amount to be split up is $125 + $18.75 = $143.75. We must now divide $143.75 by 5 to get the amount each person will contribute toward the bill: the answer is $28.75. (Note that you can estimate these figures if you are doing this in your head. For

108

instance, round the tip to $20 and divide $145 by 5 to get an answer of $29.)

Strategy (b): $125 divided by 5 is $25, the amount each person owes for the dinner without the tip. The tip is 15% of $25 = $25 x 0.15 = $3.75. Thus, each person should pay $25 + $3.75 = $28.75.

Step 5. Answer the question.

In an arithmetic problem, you have found the answer in Step 4. State the answer clearly and include any units (dollar sign, miles per hour, pounds, and so on).

In an algebra problem, once you solve the equation for the variable (x let's say), that number may or may not be the answer to the question, though it often is. Go back to Step 2b to find the question and use your solution to the equation (either directly or indirectly) to answer the question. Here, too, be sure to include the units.

Example:
As we found above, each person should pay $28.75.

Step 6. Check your answer.

Be sure that you have answered the question that is asked in the problem and that your answer makes sense. Ask yourself if your answer is too large or too small and if it has the right unit of measurement. Redo your calculations to check for accuracy (or do it an alternative way to see that you get the same answer).

For an algebra problem, you can also check that you solved an equation correctly by plugging the number you found back into the variable in the equation. You should ask yourself if the equation makes sense and accurately represents the ideas in the problem.

Example:

Strategy (a)   Redo the first two calculations and check the division by multiplying 5 x $28.75 = $143.75.

Strategy (b)   Check the division by multiplying 5 x $25 = $125 and redo the other calculations.

The following problems are provided for you to practice using the six steps to solving a word problem. The first is an arithmetic problem and the second is an algebra problem, so choose one or both, according to your level. There is discussion with each step to help guide you along.

Arithmetic Word Problem

Suppose you want to know the number of miles to the gallon your new car is getting. If you fill up the gas tank with 8 gallons of gas after having traveled 200 miles, how many miles to the gallon are you getting?

Step 1.   Identify the type of problem.

YOURS:

_____

_____

Discussion:

This problem deals with finding gas mileage.

Step 2.   Get a grasp of the problem.
   a. Look up or figure out unfamiliar words or concepts.
   b. Write down the question in words.
   c. Write down all the given information.
   d. Draw a diagram or sketch, if possible.
   e. If you are using algebra, identify the variable(s) in words.

YOURS:

a.
_____

b.
_____

c.
_____

d.

e.
_____

Discussion:

    a. If you were unfamiliar with the concept of gas mileage, you would have to learn this before you could do the problem.

    b. Find the number of miles that the car gets for each gallon of gas that the car uses.

    c. The car traveled 200 miles. It used 8 gallons of gas.

    d.

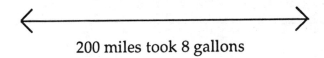

200 miles took 8 gallons

    e. This problem can be done using arithmetic.

Step 3. **Determine a strategy.**

YOURS:

_____

_____

_____

_____

Discussion:

Sometimes using either smaller or more convenient numbers in a problem helps to figure out the correct strategy. For instance, this problem seems easier if you pretend to have filled up the tank with 10 gallons of gas after having traveled for 200 miles. It may be more intuitive to come up with the answer of 20 miles per gallon, using these numbers. How did we come up with 20? We took 200 and divided it by 10. Using the same operation, division of miles by gallons, we can find the answer to the original problem.

Step 4. **Use the strategy to work the problem.**

YOURS:

_____

_____

_____

_____

Discussion:

200 divided by 8 is 25.

Step 5. Answer the question.

YOURS:

_____

Discussion:

The car gets 25 miles per gallon.

Step 6.   Check your answer.

YOURS:

_____

_____

Discussion:

If you multiply, 25 miles per gallon x 8 gallons = 200 miles. Both the numbers and the units check. Also, 25 mpg is a reasonable figure for the gas mileage.

Algebraic Word Problem

A rectangle has length which is one inch more than twice its width. If the perimeter of the rectangle is 20 inches, what is the area of the rectangle?

Step 1.   Identify the type of problem.

YOURS:

_____

_____

Discussion:

This is a geometric problem since it involves a rectangle.

Step 2.   Get a grasp of the problem.
*   a. Look up or figure out unfamiliar words or concepts.*
*   b. Write down the question in words.*
*   c. Write down all given information.*
*   d. Draw a diagram or sketch, if possible.*
*   e. If you are using algebra, identify the variable(s) in words.*

YOURS:

a.
_____

b.
_____

c.
_____

d.

e.
_____

Discussion:

    a. If the words rectangle, perimeter, or area are unfamiliar, this is the time to have them defined. Make sure you understand them all before proceeding!

    b. Find the _area_ of the rectangle.

    c. The perimeter $P = 20$ inches; $L = 2W + 1$.

    d.

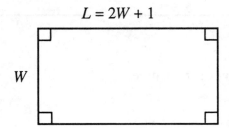

$A = L \cdot W$ (known formula)
$P = 2L + 2W$ (known formula)
$P = 20$ (given information)

    e. Let W = width of rectangle and L = length of rectangle.

Step 3.   **_Write an equation._**

YOURS:

_____

_____

_____

Discussion:

Both the perimeter and the area of a rectangle appear to be relevant formulas, namely $P = 2L + 2W$ and $A = L \cdot W$. How can we use the given information to write an equation that will help us answer the question?

If you like, try guessing at the dimensions of the rectangle, say $W = 2$ and $L = 6$. What do you notice about this guess? Well, the perimeter of such a rectangle would be 16; but the problem requires the perimeter to be 20. If we change our guess to $W = 2$ and $L = 8$, we do get $P = 20$; but the problem requires that the length be one more than twice the width. So we must look for W and L such that $P = 20$ _and_ $L = 2W + 1$. Going through this guessing process has helped us to better understand the relationships in this problem and will help us find an appropriate equation.

Since we are given that $L = 2W + 1$, we can substitute it in the formula for the perimeter. The perimeter $P = 2L + 2W$ becomes $P = 2(2W + 1) + 2W$. We are also given that $P = 20$. Thus we can write the equation in a single variable: $20 = 2(2W + 1) + 2W$.

Step 4. **_Solve the equation for W._**

YOURS:

_____

_____

_____

_____

_____

_____

Discussion:

We use the procedure for solving a linear equation.

$$20 = 2(2W + 1) + 2W$$
$$20 = 4W + 2 + 2W$$
$$20 = 6W + 2$$
$$18 = 6W$$
$$W = 3$$

Step 5. *Answer the question.*

YOURS:

_____

_____

_____

Discussion:

We found $W = 3$. Thus L = $2W + 1 = 2(3) + 1 = 7$. The question asks for the area of the rectangle. To find the *area*, $A = L \cdot W$ becomes $A = 7(3) = 21$. Therefore the area of the rectangle is 21 square inches.

Step 6. *Check your answer.*

YOURS:

_____

_____

_____

_____

_____

Discussion:

Note that the 20 on the left side of the equation gives the perimeter and the right side of the equation also describes the perimeter. Both sides of the equation match!

We found $W = 3$. We can plug 3 in for W in the equation to see if we solved the equation correctly:

$$20 = 2(2 \cdot 3 + 1) + 2 \cdot 3$$
$$20 = 2(7) + 6$$
$$20 = 14 + 6$$
$$20 = 20$$

We can check that a rectangle with dimensions $W = 3$ and $L = 7$ satisfies the conditions of the problem. $P = 20$ since $P = 2L + 2W = 2(7) + 2(3) = 20$. Also, $L = 2W + 1$ since $7 = 2(3) + 1$.

Word problems can be practiced just like other math problems. After a while, surprising as it might be, you will find that some word problems are easy! Familiarity with the type of problem, faith in your ability to solve word problems, knowledge that they take time and creativity, and perseverance all contribute to your success at solving word problems. Keep in mind, too, that the more practiced you are, the better you will do in a test situation if a word problem comes up.

CONCLUSION

Problem-solving skills are not only important in solving math problems, but in daily living. Not only are you learning mathematics, you are learning to sharpen your discrimination, observation, memorization, logic, and creative skills. As you improve in all of these areas, we hope that your confidence will continue to grow and that you will begin to enjoy math much more.

Chapter 8

Gaining Control of Time

Now that you have learned better study habits and improved your problem-solving skills, it is important to set some time aside to practice. Do you have difficulty finding time to do your math homework? Have you ever found yourself saying, "I don't know where the time goes!" or "I just don't have enough time!"

We live in a society where time is important. People tend to keep busy schedules, sometimes juggling work, school, and children. These commitments take a great amount of time and energy. Work or school begins at a specific time; we have deadlines to meet, and even in our leisure, we must make specific plans to meet people or go to the movies.

We've all heard ourselves say, "If only I could find another hour in the day!" Well, in a way, you can find another hour in the day, through gaining control of your time. And just think what you could do with that extra hour! You could visit a friend, read, or even study math. Feeling like you have gained another hour is actually only one of many benefits from gaining control of your time.

Gaining control of your time will in fact give you time to do what is important. Being in control means setting priorities and recognizing that in some situations, not *everything* can be done. You choose what is important and *make* the time for it. If you make math a priority, then you *will* find the time to devote to your math studies.

Knowing that you have set aside time for what you need and/or want to do will make you feel more relaxed. Worries such as "Oh gosh, when am I ever going to do my math homework?" will begin to disappear. You'll hear yourself say, "Oh yes, I've planned to do my math homework at 3:00 p.m. today."

The fourth benefit is that you will experience better concentration. How many times have you been doing some math homework and begun to think about a zillion and one other things that you need to do? If you have set aside the time to do the other things, then you will be able to put those thoughts aside and focus all of your energy on math. You can concentrate, knowing full well that you will get to the other activities "all in good time!"

Last, but definitely not least, being in control of your time is very empowering. It is wonderful to feel that you are actually governing your time, as opposed to it governing you. You'll no longer be saying "I don't know where the time went," but rather "I spent my time as I planned!"

HOW YOU SPEND TIME

In order to gain control of your time, it is essential to evaluate how you spend your time *now* and look at ways that you might "waste time."

A study skills class was asked to record how they spent their time for an entire week. One particular student, Doris, had been complaining that she didn't have enough time to complete her homework assignments. After looking at her week's activities, Doris discovered why she didn't have enough time for homework. Look over her schedule. Can you tell where the time went?

Doris's schedule

<u>Schedule</u>　　　　Name　_Doris_

Week of:	THURSDAY	FRIDAY	SATURDAY
6 a.m.	sleep	sleep	
7 a.m.	get ready	get ready	
8 a.m.	for school	for school	sleep
9 a.m.	ENGL 101	MATH 100	
10 a.m.	SOC 103	PSYC 121	
11 a.m.	lunch in	lunch	watch
12 p.m.	student center		cartoons
1 p.m.	watch TV	As The World Turns	MTV
2 p.m.	General Hospital	General Hospital	saturday afternoon movies
3 p.m.	Oprah Winfrey	Oprah Winfrey	
4 p.m.	go home	go home	
5 p.m.	relax	relax	
6 p.m.	Dinner	Dinner	Dinner
7 p.m.		Geraldo	talk on phone
8 p.m.	The Simpsons	go out	homework
9 p.m.	Star Trek		watch TV
10 p.m.	study		scary movie
11p.m.	go to bed		
12-2 a.m.			
2-4 a.m.	sleep		sleep
4-6 a.m.			

Doris discovered she really *didn't* have time for homework because she was too busy watching television. When she took the time out to record what she was doing during the day, the television addiction hit her smack in the face. She was no longer able to hide from the fact that she spent her time unwisely.

Now it's your turn to look at how you spend your time. For the next two days record exactly what you do and when. The best way keep track is to record your activities every hour for the previous 60 minutes. BE HONEST. We hope that your schedule will not be as devastating as Doris's, but that you will learn more about your own use of time. This is a wonderful opportunity to see how you spend and how you waste your time. Please note that we have included a sample schedule on the next page.

OTHERS:

Week of:	MONDAY	TUESDAY
6 a.m.	sleep wake up, shower	sleep wake up, shower
7 a.m.	get kids up, make breakfast	get kids up, make breakfast
8 a.m.	take kids to school in transit to work	take kids to school, in transit to work
9 a.m.	work	work
10 a.m.	"	"
11 a.m.	"	"
12 p.m.	lunch	lunch with Gary
1 p.m.	drive to school visit with friends	lunch with Gary
2 p.m.	English class	late for Sociology class
3 p.m.	Math class	coffee with friends in student union
4 p.m.	pick up kids grocery store	play racquetball pick up kids
5 p.m.	visit with kids, start dinner	dry cleaners, start dinner
6 p.m.	eat dinner	eat dinner
7 p.m.	talk w/ Jeannie on phone, TV	help kids with homework
8 p.m.	iron dress, kids to bed	kids for ice cream, to bed
9 p.m.	study	talk on phone to Gary
10 p.m.	talk on phone to Gary	watch TV
11 p.m.	study	TV
12 a.m.	study	go to bed
1 a.m.	go to bed	sleep

YOURS:

Week of:	WEEKDAY #1	WEEKDAY #2
6 a.m.		
7 a.m.		
8 a.m.		
9 a.m.		
10 a.m.		
11 a.m.		
12 p.m.		
1 p.m.		
2 p.m.		
3 p.m.		
4 p.m.		
5 p.m.		
6 p.m.		
7 p.m.		
8 p.m.		
9 p.m.		
10 p.m.		
11 p.m.		
12 a.m.		
1 a.m.		

Take a good look at your schedule for the last two days. What did you learn about how you spent your time? What are your general impressions? Are there long periods of wasted time? Were there things that you wished you had found the time to do?

OTHERS:

It looks like I'm trying to do too much.

I talked on the phone too much.

I don't have enough unplanned time to myself.

I visit with people too long.

YOURS:

_____

_____

_____

_____

_____

_____

MAKING A SCHEDULE

If you were not pleased with how you spent your time in the previous exercise, then you need to learn to take control of your time. Time management involves planning your days so that you can accomplish the things you want and need to do. Begin by thinking about your next three days. You already have some commitments. You have to be at work or at school at a specific time. You have agreed to meet a friend for dinner on Wednesday, or to attend an aerobics class at 5:30 p.m. on Monday and Wednesday. These are called your "fixed time commitments." They consist of anything that you *know* you have to do, and you know *exactly when you have to do it*.

Please take a few minutes to list all of your fixed time commitments. Take care in also listing exactly what day and time these commitments are scheduled.

OTHERS:

ACTIVITY	TIME	DAY
___work	8:00 a.m.-12:00 p.m.	Mon. & Wed.
___babysitting	7:00 p.m.-11:30 p.m.	Tuesday
___classes	2:00 p.m.-4:00 p.m.	Mon., Wed. & Fri.
___dinner date	7:00 p.m.- ??	Wednesday

YOURS:

ACTIVITY	TIME	DAY

_____

_____

_____

_____

_____

_____

_____

Look at the schedule on p. 129. Your fixed time commitments are the first things to fill in on your schedule because you know when you have to do them. Take a few minutes to fill them in the appropriate time slots in the schedule. You can do this in ink, since these times are fixed. Be sure to check off each of the commitments on your list when you place it on the schedule.

Now that your schedule includes your fixed time commitments, you can look at how you will spend the rest of your time. You will need a pencil, instead of a pen, to complete this part of the exercise, since you may be making changes. Start by making a list of the things you *need* to do. These will be things you *need* to do, but are *not* prescheduled at a specific time. Some examples of this "must do" category might be math homework, work in this book, grocery shopping, clean the house, laundry, or write a letter to a friend.

Take a minute to make a list of the must do's and assign them a day and time. You'll need to assess how long each of these activities will take.

OTHERS:

THINGS I NEED TO DO	AMOUNT OF TIME	DAY(S)
___ clean house	40 minutes	Mon., 3:00 p.m.
___ read this book	40 min./per day	Mon. & Wed., 1:00 p.m.
___ laundry	1 hour	Tues., 7:00 p.m.

YOURS:

THINGS I NEED TO DO	AMOUNT OF TIME	DAY(S)

_____

_____

_____

_____

_____

_____

_____

_____

_____

After you have made your list, be sure to place the "must do's" in the schedule on p. 129. After each one is written in the appropriate time slot on the schedule, check off the activity.

You now have all of the things you "should do" in your schedule—the fixed time commitments and the must do's. It's finally time to think about having fun. This last category is called "me time." "Me time" stands for all the things that you *want* to do—time for relaxation, time to play ball with friends, time to talk on the phone, time to visit friends, and time to just have for yourself. List all of the fun things that you want to do in the next three days. Take a minute to evaluate how much time will be needed for each activity and on what day you would like to do it.

OTHERS:

THINGS I WANT TO DO	AMOUNT OF TIME	DAY(S)
___ relaxation	20 mins. per day	Mon. Tue. & Wed.
___ read	1 hr. for 2 days	Wed. & Thur.
___ call Mark	30 minutes	Tuesday

YOURS:

THINGS I WANT TO DO	AMOUNT OF TIME	DAY(S)

_____

_____

_____

_____

_____

_____

_____

After you have made your list, be sure to place your me times on your schedule. Be sure to check off each activity after you have placed it on the schedule.

<u>Schedule</u>   Name_____

Week of:	Day 1	Day 2	Day3
6 a.m.			
7 a.m.			
8 a.m.			
9 a.m.			
10 a.m.			
11 a.m.			
12 p.m.			
1 p.m.			
2 p.m.			
3 p.m.			
4 p.m.			
5 p.m.			
6 p.m.			
7 p.m.			
8 p.m.			
9 p.m.			
10 p.m.			
11 p.m.			
12-2 a.m.			
2-4 a.m.			
4-6 a.m.			

Now that you have written your schedule for the next three days, try to follow it as closely as possible. At the end of each day, look over your schedule and make note of how you diverged from your plan, if at all.

What did you do differently from your schedule?

OTHERS:

Monday:	I did not clean the house.
Tuesday:	I did not read this book.
Wednesday:	I did everything that was on my schedule, and I had plenty of time to relax as well.

YOURS:

_____

_____

_____

_____

_____

_____

_____

_____

You may find that changes you made from your original schedule were changes that you *wanted* to make. Something that you wanted to do may have come up and consequently you did something other than what was scheduled. If you felt comfortable with these changes, then you must have set the new activity as a priority over the scheduled one. You were flexible enough to recognize which activity was more important to you, and you made the adjustment.

If you made the changes but *didn't* feel comfortable, then you might want to either (1) not divert from your original schedule next time, or (2) be sure when writing a new schedule to include enough free time to accommodate an unplanned activity.

CONCLUSION

Time management is a never-ending process of scheduling and rescheduling. Initially, to be assured of having the time to work at overcoming math anxiety, you will actually need to write down and follow a schedule. Eventually, as you become more aware of your time and the process of scheduling time, you will find that you can plan your days in a less formal way.

Remember that becoming math anxiety free requires time. It takes time to work through this book, time to relax, and time to study. If overcoming math anxiety is important to you, then you can take control and **make the time!**

Chapter 9

Staying Math Anxiety Free

You are now coming to the end of your guided journey to becoming math anxiety free. You have traveled the roads we set forth and hopefully felt the excitement of learning new things about yourself and new ways to deal with your math anxiety. We hope that you have had some positive experiences and successes with math since you started work on conquering your math anxiety. We hope that you have been gaining some confidence and will continue to do so as you practice the techniques presented in this book. In reflecting on your journey to becoming free of math anxiety, take a few moments to think about your accomplishments.

Since you started working in this book, what positive experiences have you had while dealing with math? How have your attitudes about math and yourself with respect to math changed? How would you now rate your anxiety level when confronted with math?

OTHERS:

One time, I got my nerve up to answer a problem at the board. Though I was nervous,
    I knew that I could do it, and was so proud when I did!
I feel less anxious when confronted with math problems.
I don't seem to give up as quickly when I can't do a problem right away.
I still get tense about word problems. But I do the quickie Relaxation Technique and even
    though I'm still worried about being able to work the problem, I feel less tense.

YOURS:

_____

_____

_____

_____

_____

_____

_____

As a conclusion to the book, let's review the topics discussed. Then we can look toward the future and how you can maintain your newly acquired skills and knowledge.

Your journey began with self-discovery. Recognizing how you personally experience math anxiety was your first stop. Putting yourself in a math anxious situation helped you become aware of your symptoms of math anxiety. If you had not been consciously aware of these symptoms, getting in touch with them may have led you to believe you were more anxious than you had realized. You quickly learned that these symptoms are actually a way to alert you to your anxiety so that you can take control and regroup, using the tools presented in this book.

A better and clearer understanding of where your math anxious feelings come from was explored in the chapter called Origins. It is important for you to understand how you became math anxious and for you to recognize that you weren't born with math anxiety. Rather, math anxiety develops in a variety of ways, including internalized messages that you have been given throughout your life. You were possibly told by a teacher that "Girls don't need to know math," or by a parent that "Your sister is the mathematician!" Your exploration of your own math history has hopefully given you insight into the reasons for feeling math anxious and the inspiration to move beyond it.

Math anxiety had been a part of your life for a long time. Your ride on the anxiety cycle merry-go-round has made you dizzy. When you have a mathematical task to perform and you start to think, "Oh no, I can't do this," you begin to feel anxious. You may exhibit signs such as sweaty palms, a racing heartbeat, and continued negative inner messages. Your anxiety distracts you and tears away your confidence so you end up with a poor performance on the mathematical task. You feel like a failure, and your inner messages confirm that feeling. Then the next time you are faced with a mathematical task, if you can prepare for it, you react in a very anxious manner: by either avoiding the preparatory work or possibly working too frantically to be able to understand what you are working on. In either case, you are not ready to face the mathematical task psychologically or mathematically. Your inner messages remind you of this and you remain caught up in the cycle.

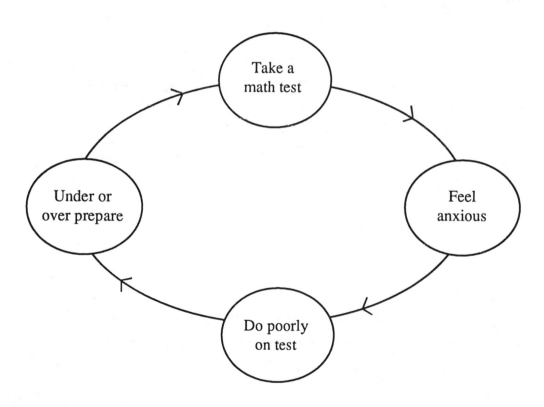

Figure 3. The anxiety cycle.

You have learned several tools for overcoming math anxiety—ways to help you get off of the anxiety cycle merry-go-round. Since inner messages keep you moving around and around the cycle, one way to break the cyclical motion is to stop those messages.

Changing negative inner messages to positive ones and using the positive messages is an excellent way to control your anxiety so that you can concentrate and perform better on mathematical tasks. Relaxation can calm you when you begin to be alerted to your math anxious symptoms. Incorporating positive inner messages into the Relaxation Technique facilitates using them when you begin to feel anxious. When preparing for a math task, particularly in a classroom setting, using better study techniques, problem-solving skills, and time management skills all help to improve your confidence and your mathematical successes. Consequently, your anxiety lessens and you have jumped off the anxiety cycle. When you break out of the anxiety cycle, you begin to walk a road free of math anxiety. (See Figure 4).

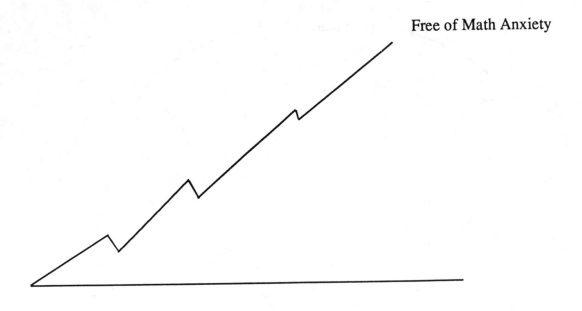

Free of Math Anxiety

Figure 4. The road to staying math anxiety free.

Since your feelings of math anxiety have been in place for many years, it would be impossible to assume that you would be totally free of math anxiety after completing this book. Along this road, you will experience some setbacks. Becoming and staying free of math anxiety is an ongoing process. It is important for you to remain conscious of the possibility of re-experiencing math anxiety and to continue using the tools you have now incorporated into your life. If at some time you experience an unpleasant situation concerning math, for example doing poorly on a math test, you may begin to doubt your abilities again, hearing yourself say "I knew that I couldn't do math!" Remember that this is only a minor setback and does not mean you are back at ground zero. You will quickly recognize that you are beginning to get caught up in that old anxiety cycle, and you will be able to stop yourself. Use this book as a resource, as a reminder of the tools that have been most effective for you. You will put yourself right back in the groove, on the road to staying math anxiety free!

Now that you have gained some confidence in your math abilities, MEET THE CHALLENGE HEAD ON! Take that math course that you were afraid to take, grab for the check at the restaurant, and volunteer to do those income taxes! MEET THE CHALLENGE! You've got the tools and the resources—*you can do it*!

Appendixes

Appendix A

Answers to quiz in Chapter 2.

1.
```
    85
  x .12
   170
   850
 10.20
```

2. $\dfrac{2}{3} - \dfrac{1}{2} = \dfrac{4}{6} - \dfrac{3}{6} = \dfrac{1}{6}$

3.

$$P = 2L + 2W = 150$$

Since: $P = 150$
we have: $2L + 2W = 150$

Since: $L = 2W$
we have: $2(2W) + 2W = 150$
$4W + 2W = 150$
$6W = 150$
$W = 25$

and $L = 2W$
$L = 2(25)$
$L = 50$

and $A = L \cdot W$
$A = (50)(25)$
$A = 1250$ sq. ft.

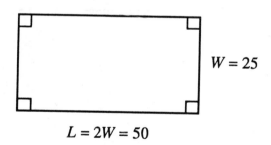

$W = 25$

$L = 2W = 50$

4.
$$2(x - 3) = -12$$
$$2x - 6 = -12$$
$$2x = -12 + 6$$
$$2x = -6$$
$$x = -3$$

5. Here's one way.

4	3	8
9	5	1
2	7	6

Appendix B

Answers to the problem set in Chapter 2.

1.   5.017
         -3.940
         1.077

2.

$$\frac{3\,(7 - 9) - 10}{5\,(3 - 4) + 1} =$$

$$= \frac{3\,(-2) - 10}{5\,(-1) + 1}$$

$$= \frac{-6 - 10}{-5 + 1}$$

$$= \frac{-16}{-4}$$

$$= 4$$

3. $A = \tfrac{1}{2}BH = \tfrac{1}{2}(10)(4) = 20$ sq. cm.

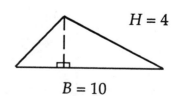

4. x = Bill's age
                    $x + 1$ = Jane's age
                       $3x$ = Father's age

$(x + 1) + x + 3x = 76$
$5x + 1 = 76$
$5x = 75$
$x = 15$

Bill is 15
Jane is 15 + 1 = 16
Father is 3(15) = 45

5.

$$\sqrt{6} + \sqrt{12} + \sqrt{24} + \sqrt{27} =$$

$$= \sqrt{6} + 2\sqrt{3} + 2\sqrt{6} + 3\sqrt{3}$$

$$= 3\sqrt{6} + 5\sqrt{3}$$

6.

$$\frac{3}{x + 1} + \frac{x}{x^2 + 2x + 1} =$$

$$= \frac{3}{x + 1} + \frac{x}{(x + 1)(x + 1)}$$

$$\text{LCD} = (x + 1)(x + 1) = (x + 1)^2$$

$$= \frac{3(x + 1)}{(x + 1)^2} + \frac{x}{(x + 1)^2}$$

$$= \frac{3(x + 1) + x}{(x + 1)^2}$$

$$= \frac{3x + 3 + x}{(x + 1)^2}$$

$$= \frac{4x + 3}{(x + 1)^2}$$

Appendix C

Math Journal   (Chapter 2)

SITUATION: _____
_____
_____
_____
_____
_____

YOUR SYMPTOMS OF ANXIETY: _____
_____
_____

WHAT ACTION DID YOU TAKE? _____
_____
_____
_____

I LEARNED THAT: _____
_____
_____
_____

Appendix D

Changing Negative Inner Messages to Positive Inner Messages (Chapter 4)

1. Choose one negative inner message that you give yourself. Write it in the space provided.

   _____

2. Write down all of the *disadvantages* of giving yourself this negative inner message.

   _____

   _____

   _____

   _____

3. Rewrite your negative inner message as a positive one.

   _____

   _____

4. What *keeps you* from using this positive inner message?

   _____

   _____

5. Write down all of the *advantages* in giving yourself this positive inner message.

   _____

   _____

   _____

   _____

   _____

   _____

   _____

Appendix E

Being Aware of Your Inner Messages *(Chapter 4)*

1. *Describe* the situation in which you were feeling anxious and were aware of your inner voice at work.

_____

_____

_____

_____

_____

2. *List* the inner messages that you gave yourself, both negative and positive.

_____

_____

_____

_____

_____

3. *Describe* your feelings and experiences that resulted from these inner messages.

_____

_____

_____

_____

_____

4. If you changed a negative inner message to a positive one, *state* both the old and the new messages and then *describe* how the change affected your experience.

_____

_____

_____

_____

_____

_____

Appendix F

Relaxation Practice Sessions   (Chapter 5)

Date _____

Time _____

Your reactions

_____

_____

_____

_____

Date _____

Time _____

Your reactions

_____

_____

_____

_____

Appendix G

Weekly Schedule (Chapter 8)

Week	MONDAY	TUESDAY	WEDNESDAY
6 a.m.			
7 a.m.			
8 a.m.			
9 a.m.			
10 a.m.			
11 a.m.			
12 p.m.			
1 p.m.			
2 p.m.			
3 p.m.			
4 p.m.			
5 p.m.			
6 p.m.			
7 p.m.			
8 p.m.			
9 p.m.			
10 p.m.			
11 p.m.			
12 a.m.			
1 a.m.			

Continued

Week	THURSDAY	FRIDAY	SAT./SUN.
6 a.m.			
7 a.m.			
8 a.m.			
9 a.m.			
10 a.m.			
11 a.m.			
12 p.m.			
1 p.m.			
2 p.m.			
3 p.m.			
4 p.m.			
5 p.m.			
6 p.m.			
7 p.m.			
8 p.m.			
9 p.m.			
10 p.m.			
11 p.m.			
12 a.m.			
1 a.m.			